RAILWAY HERITAGE

PADDINGTON

Great Western Gateway

5
4

RAILWAY HERITAGE

PADDINGTON

Great Western Gateway

A portrait of the 'aristocrat' of London's railway termini

Tim Bryan

Silver Link Publishing Ltd

First published in October 1997
Reprinted September 1999

British Library Cataloguing in Publication Data

A catalogue record for this book is available from the British Library

ISBN 1 85794 102 0

Silver Link Publishing Ltd
The Trundle
Ringstead Road
Great Addington
Kettering
Northants
NN14 4BW

Tel/Fax: 01536 330588
email: sales@slinkp-p.demon.co.uk

Printed and bound in Great Britain

Frontispiece **Passengers walking down towards the 'Lawn' in about 1983.**

ACKNOWLEDGEMENTS

I am grateful for the assistance of a number of individuals and institutions for their assistance in the compilation of this volume, and for permission to reproduce illustrations. I would also like to acknowledge the assistance and support of my family, particularly my wife Ann, who put up with my absences while I finished the book.

Thanks are due to: Ian Coulson, David Ellis and Jack Hayward, and particularly to David Hyde for his work in identifying many of the pictures that have come from the GWR Museum collection and his detailed knowledge of the station and its history. I would also like to acknowledge the assistance of Linda Huig at Leicester University Library, and also the staff at Swindon Reference Library. Assistance regarding more recent developments at the station has kindly been given by Railtrack Corporate Affairs, London, and from Clive Hammond, Public Affairs Manager, Railtrack Great Western, and Elaine Wild, from the press office of Great Western Trains. Others who made material available were Mrs J. McLeod, Mrs M. Roberts and Mr K. Kirkpatrick, who kindly made his late father's collection of wartime views available. Thanks are also due to Dick Riley, who allowed me to use pictures from his collection.

Photographs from the GWR Museum collection are reproduced by courtesy of Swindon Borough Council, and I am also grateful for the assistance of Dieter Hopkin, Curator of the 2D Collections at the National Railway Museum at York, for permission to use material from their collection.

In some cases it was not possible to identify the source of photographs, and apologies are tendered in advance to anyone I have omitted to credit; those that can be identified are as follows:

B. Arman Collection: 80
J. Davenport: 44 (l)
Great Western Trains Company: 13 (l), 107-109, 110-111
GWR Museum/Swindon Museums Collection: 10, 11, 13, 16 (upper), 17, 20 (lower), 21, 22, 24 (u), 25 (l), 26 (l), 36 (l), 37, 38, 39, 42 (u), 46 (l), 48, 49, 50, 51, 53 (u)-55, 65 (l), 67, 70-72, 74, 76-77, 83-85, 87, 104-105, 106 (u)
National Railway Museum, York: 8, 15, 18, 19, 20 (u), 23, 24 (l), 26 (u), 27, 31, 32, 33, 52, 57, 59, 64, 69, 75, 78, 81, 82
Kirkpatrick Collection: 12 (l), 16 (l), 48 (u), 58, 65, 68, 93, 96 (l), 97-101
Leicester University Library Collection: 25 (u), 28-29, 42 (l), 53 (all), 56, 60-62, 86, 92 (l), 94-96, 102-103
Lens of Sutton: 30 (both), 36 (u), 92 (u)
Mrs J. McLeod: 66
Railway Gazette International: 88-89
R. C. Riley: 41, 46, 47
Stations Ltd: 106 (l)
All other illustrations are from the author's collection.

CONTENTS

FOREWORD

by
Brian Scott OBE
Chief Executive, Great Western Holdings

Tim Bryan rightly commands considerable respect for his extensive knowledge of the Great Western Railway and I am delighted, both personally and as Chief Executive of Great Western Holdings, to commend his latest publication to all who share his affection for the heritage of the GWR and its London terminus, Paddington station.

The evocative illustrations he has selected cover the period from the end of the Broad Gauge to the present day and the emergence of Great Western Trains as the proud successor to the GWR tradition. Tim Bryan is to be congratulated on bringing such a magnificent feature of our national transport history to life in such a vivid and appealing way. I regard it as a privilege to endorse this book.

INTRODUCTION

Paddington station, the Great Western Railway boasted in its 1928 edition of 'Holiday Haunts', 'is one of the finest railway stations in London - the aristocrat amongst the railway termini of the metropolis'. Hopefully, this volume will give the reader something of an impression of why the GWR was so proud of its largest and arguably most famous station.

No attempt has been made to give a detailed history of Paddington, a task that would take up far more space than is available in this book, and something that has been done in a number of worthy books and articles, most notably within the pages of the Great Western's own company magazine over many years. This book therefore is a collection of photographs, attempting to distil the essence of what Paddington was and is, to the railway, its staff and passengers. Some of the pictures shown will be familiar, others hopefully will not.

In historical terms the book covers broadly what might be called the 'modern era' of the station, namely the years after the abolition of Brunel's broad gauge in 1892 up to the present day; I have tried to reflect most of the major developments and events that have affected the fortunes of the station, but have also aimed to tell something of the story of the staff and passengers who have played such an important part of the history of Paddington.

Readers will also notice that I have tried to concentrate my survey on the station and its immediate surroundings, and thus Royal Oak station is the limit of the our 'photographer's permit'. The history of Paddington's locomotive depot at Old Oak Common has been told in some detail elsewhere, so lovers of the Great Western steam locomotive will have to be content with views of Swindon products taken rather nearer the buffer stops at Paddington!

Despite almost continuous improvement, enlargement and development at the terminus since its construction in 1854, Paddington even today retains many of the original features of Isambard Kingdom Brunel's design. Much has changed since those early days; the broad gauge favoured by the great engineer himself was abolished in 1892, and the station has witnessed the dramatic growth and development of first steam then diesel power. Today it is moving towards the Millennium ready to welcome electric trains; overhead catenary wires herald the new 'Heathrow Express' services, the kind of new railway development the station's creator would surely have approved of. As Paddington moves into the next century, its title as the 'aristocrat' of London's railway stations is certainly still deserved, and it is to be hoped that by the time of its bicentenary in 2054 it will still be the premier station on 'God's Wonderful Railway'.

Left Perhaps the classic view of Paddington taken just before the Great War. The scene looking down the length of platform 1 is a busy one, and the large three-sided clock shows that the time is 11.10. The original clockwork mechanism of this Paddington landmark was replaced in 1928 by a 'pulsynetic' electric system run by a master clock, which also ran clocks on the 'Lawn' and the approach road. The Dean Clerestory coach coupled to the rear of the train contrasts strongly with the more modern 'Toplight' stock at the front. In the foreground two ladies are busy talking to one of the many porters to be seen loading luggage on to the train.

A BRIEF HISTORY OF PADDINGTON STATION

Since this volume will deal primarily with the station in the 20th century, it would be useful to set the scene by giving the reader an outline of the history of the terminus from its earliest days to the present, in order to give some historical perspective to the photographs that will follow.

A number of locations were suggested for the London terminus of Brunel's Great Western Railway when it was being planned in the 1830s, including Brentford, Hammersmith and Acton, but it was not until the Great Western Act of Parliament, which was passed on 31 August 1835, that provision was made for the GWR to construct a junction with the London & Birmingham Railway to enable the two railways to share a terminus at Euston. This rather uneasy partnership was doomed to failure, and the scheme soon foundered over disagreements regarding land at Camden and Euston, but more significantly over the decision taken by the GWR Directors in October 1835 to adopt Brunel's 'Broad Gauge' of 7 ft 0¼ in. The operating difficulties envisaged by the London & Birmingham would eventually return to haunt the Great Western too, but in the meantime in July 1837 parliamentary permission was given to build over 4 miles of new line from Acton to a location next to the canal at Paddington.

The first station at Paddington was probably never seen as anything but temporary; certainly lack of finance

A map originally reproduced in the *Great Western Railway Magazine*, which shows the sites of the 1838 and 1854 stations, and an impression of the landscape in which the railway was originally built.

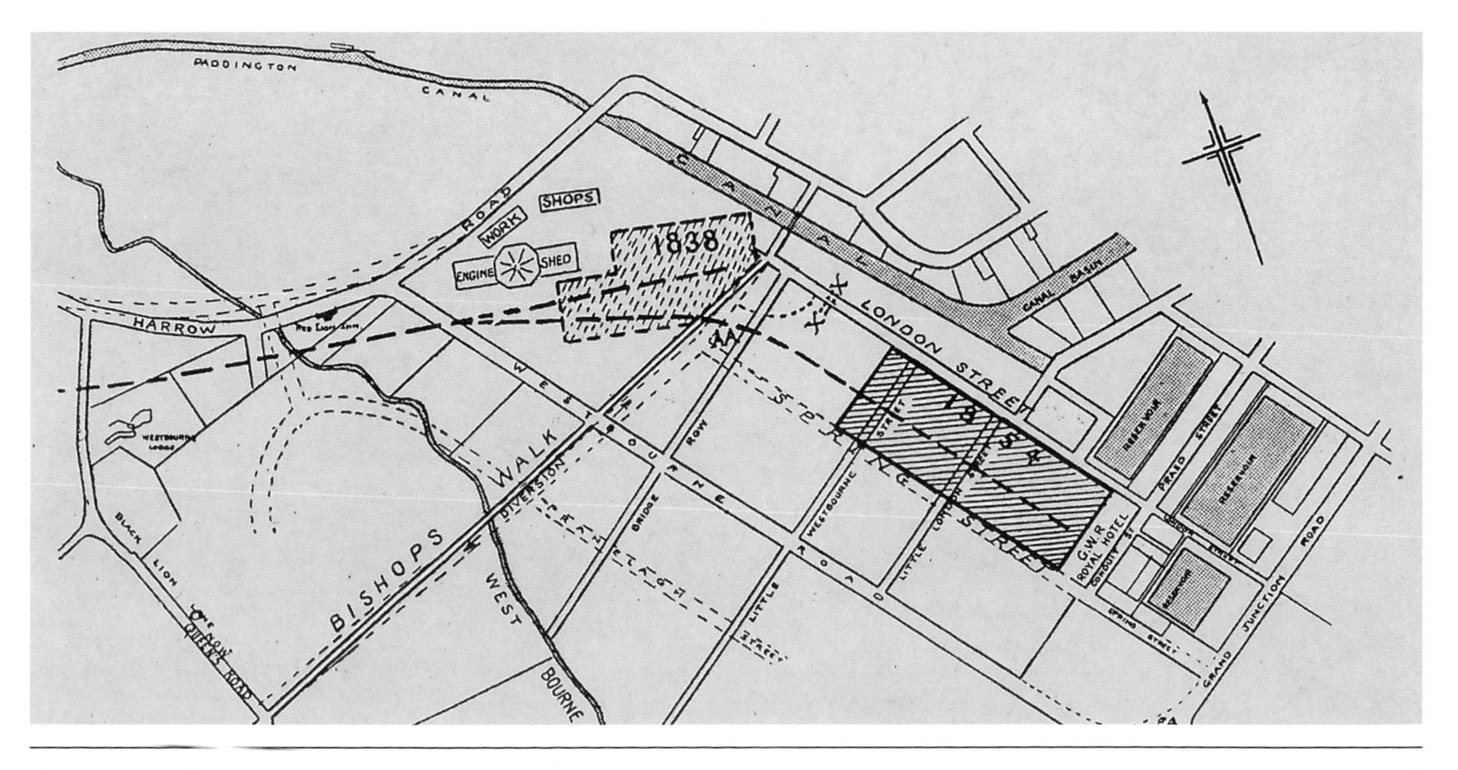

Something of the semi rural nature of Paddington in the early days of its history can be seen in this lithograph by J. C. Bourne.
The first station was situated beyond the arches of the bridge.

The artist of this lithograph of Paddington in 1874 is not known, but he has certainly captured something of the hustle and bustle of the terminus in the Broad Gauge era! The use of the station walls for advertising is of interest, with all manner of products being promoted.

prevented Brunel from building the grand station he had in mind for some years, and the new terminus was a small affair, with only four platforms, and consisting of a plain wooden-roofed train shed that was a far cry from the extensive new station built by the railway at Bristol.

By the early 1850s traffic on the Great Western had increased, and pressure on the old station was becoming intolerable. Brunel was therefore finally able to design a building that was of a scale and quality to match the rest of the railway. The great station was brought fully into use on 29 May 1854 and consisted of three impressive wrought iron arched roof spans supported by cast iron columns. The train shed was 700 feet long and 238 feet wide, and when opened had ten tracks, of which only five were platform lines; the remaining five were used for the storage of rolling-stock. In his designs for the station Brunel had been much influenced by the work of Joseph Paxton on the 'Crystal Palace' for the Great Exhibition of 1851, and he utilised Paxton's 'patent glazing' for the roof lights; he also employed his friend, the architect Matthew Digby Wyatt, to design the ironwork for the glass screens at the Bristol end of the station.

The stunning design proved more than adequate for over 40 years, when traffic had increased to the point where more dramatic extensions to the station were to prove necessary. Up until this point expansion had taken place through the removal of the previously mentioned carriage sidings, and their replacement with platforms; in 1878 platform 9 was added, and in 1884 platforms 4 and 5. Standard gauge tracks were first laid in the station in 1861, when services from newly acquired lines in the West Midlands began to run to the capital. After the abolition of the broad gauge in 1892 yet another platform was added by the removal of a carriage line.

In the years before the Great War more dramatic changes took place. Improvements to the railway under its dynamic General Manager James Inglis, such as the opening of 'cut off' lines shortening the route to the West, the development of Fishguard Harbour and an influx of new and powerful locomotives designed by G. J. Churchward, led to an upturn in passenger business with which Brunel's great station could not cope. A new roof span, this time built of steel instead of wrought iron, was added, construction being completed in 1915. Extensive alterations were also made to the track layout around the station, which also involved the demolition of a number of brick-arched bridges between Paddington and Old Oak Common, where a new locomotive depot had also been opened in 1906.

Between the two World Wars further expansion of the station took place; access to Government funds intended to alleviate unemployment allowed the company to modernise the station still further. A new parcels department was built, and platforms were extended to accommodate longer trains. The circulating area known as the 'Lawn' (so named since it was originally built on land that contained a number of cottages with gardens) was dramatically improved.

Linked by a footbridge from the main station was Bishop's Road, which served the Metropolitan Railway's line into the City of London; this opened in 1863 and was

Above A classic postcard view of the station, posted on 24 March 1914. The crowds evident in the picture suggest that it may have been taken on a busy summer Saturday or Bank Holiday.

Below The effects of the Blitz at Paddington. This is the scene at 8.00 am on 17 April 1941 in the departure road in Eastbourne Terrace after a parachute mine had hit the offices at 2.45 am that morning.

Above The BR Standard era: 'Britannia' Class 4-6-2 No 70026 *Polar Star* leaves Paddington on the down 'Red Dragon' express in June 1959.

Below A British Rail Western Region High Speed Train waits under Brunel's great roof on the evening of 20 December 1987. In the background another set waits in the older yellow and blue Intercity livery.

initially operated by the Great Western on a broad gauge basis. After a short period it was taken over by the Metropolitan, with whom the Great Western jointly built the Hammersmith & City line a short time later. This railway ran away from Bishop's Road, into the growing West London suburbs. By 1933 the demands of suburban traffic meant that Bishop's Road was ripe for redevelopment, and it was extensively rebuilt, losing its name shortly after. Resignalling and further alterations to the track layout both in the station at Paddington and on the lines running towards Old Oak Common also continued in the interwar period. The 1930s also saw the extension of the offices that were grouped around both the arrival and departure sides of the station, as well as the modernisation of the Great Western Royal Hotel, which, dating from 1852, was one of the best in the capital for many years.

Many of the most dramatic improvements suggested in a 1929 report on the future of the station were not carried out due to lack of capital and ultimately the outbreak of war, but by 1939 Paddington was a modern station with some of the best passenger facilities anywhere in the country. The Blitz took its toll of the station, although Brunel's great roof was fortunate and escaped with only one major hit in 1944 when a 500 kg bomb broke one of the roof ribs. Elsewhere within the station precinct there were over 400 incidents during the war, and GWR ARP and Rescue squads played a vital part in protecting the station and its passengers.

Postwar austerity prevented much more development taking place at Paddington, and it was not until after the demise of steam in the 1960s that more substantial work took place to update the station. Its layout was not conducive to flexible working, since there was a strict division of platforms between departures (1 to 4) and arrivals (7 to 11). In the latter part of 1967 both the trackwork and signalling of the terminus were remodelled to allow 'in and out' working to all platforms. More recently the Lawn area was extended by the shortening of platforms; other developments included the provision of a new large train indicator, a new Travel Centre, and refurbishment of catering facilities. Perhaps the most important work to be carried out in recent years has been the complete restoration of Brunel's roof, which took several years, but has ensured the survival of the station for the foreseeable future, and has greatly improved its overall appearance.

At the time of writing further dramatic changes were taking place, with building work taking place on platforms 8 and 9 for the provision of new facilities for the 'Heathrow Express' services due to commence in 1998. The new high-speed line to Heathrow Airport will use electric stock, and overhead wires and gantries are now part of the station scenery. The introduction of such an innovation might not be so revolutionary, since the Great Western had considered electrifying its own lines as far back as 1930! What the new scheme does demonstrate, however, is that the original concept and design envisaged by Brunel for Paddington has been sturdy enough to accommodate all the demands placed upon it over the years, and the station should continue to serve passengers for some time yet.

1. WELCOME TO PADDINGTON

Eastbourne Terrace

The first of three contrasting views shows the departure side of Paddington adjacent to Eastbourne Terrace, probably taken just after the First World War. Taxi cabs are pulling into the station and the clock on the ornate arch shows that it is 10.25 am, almost too late for any passengers for the 'Cornish Riviera Limited', which will be leaving in 5 minutes. There is a huge variety of traffic to be seen in Eastbourne Terrace - buses, lorries and a horse-drawn wagon all jostle for position in the busy street. On the extreme right of the picture can be seen the side of the Great Western Hotel, and the roof of Brunel's train shed is visible between the hotel and the large four-storey Office building. A small florist's shop stands at the front of the rather untidy entrance area; the single-storey area behind it was to be replaced by additional offices in the 1930s.

Above A closer view of the departure side of the station taken in 1938. The elaborate arch is very similar to one constructed at Windsor station and was probably built in the 1890s. In the previous picture it was adorned with the company coat of arms, but this has now been replaced by the 'shirt button' monogram adopted by the Great Western in the 1930s. Under the long entrance awning, porters and other station staff await the arrival of passengers, and a number of sack trucks can be seen ready for use.

The banner hanging over the entrance refers to a campaign waged by all the 'Big Four' railway companies to try and get fairer treatment for railways against the encroachment of road transport competition.

Left Strictly speaking, this photograph is out of the general sequence of pictures. However it is useful to show how the view along Eastbourne Terrace changed through the effects of the Blitz of the Second World War. Further photographs of bomb damage will be featured later in this volume, but here the devastation wrought by Nazi bombers can clearly be seen; the departure arch on the right has gone, and only the skeletal frame of the awning remains (see also the photograph on page 12).

Taken on Saturday 12 August 1944, the photograph shows crowds of passengers queuing for trains, the photographer recording that the tail of the queue was actually in Westbourne Terrace via Craven Road. Despite all the efforts of the Government and the railways to try and persuade people to stay at home, tired Londoners, worn down by almost five years of war and more recent V-1 'flying bomb' attacks, flocked to the station. On the previous Saturday pressure had been so great that the GWR had been forced to close the station for 3 hours, the first time such a thing had happened there. The Ministry of Transport resolutely refused the allow extra trains to be run, a situation only changed when the GWR's General Manager contacted the Prime Minister's Office personally to complain.

Buying a ticket

The Ticket Office was extensively modernised as part of substantial improvements made at Paddington between the wars. This photograph was taken in May 1936 and shows the rather cleaner lines of the No 2 Booking Hall. The spaces between the five ticket windows was filled with GWR posters. Not surprisingly, two advertise Cornwall, while the others feature Devon and Herefordshire.

Above Before modernisation, the Ticket Office at Paddington was a grand affair, with oak and mahogany panelling in the public areas. The scene behind the public area was, however, rather less grand, as this 1913 view shows; in the foreground a ticket clerk is stamping the date on one of the thousands of Edmondson card tickets to be seen in the racks. Given the large number of different ticket and journey types, one can imagine that the staff must have had an almost encyclopedic knowledge of the company's services and lines. Three further staff can be seen in the gloom, which the electric lighting does not seem to be alleviating!

Passenger facilities

Having purchased a ticket for their Great Western journey, the passengers might well wish not to stand on the bustling platforms at Paddington, particularly during the winter months. This photograph records the scene inside the First Class Waiting Room in 1912. Company advertising before the Great War was rather more restrained than in later years, and it is restricted here to the framed photographs of 'Places of Interest' hanging on the wall; strangely enough, the large framed picture on the right-hand side of the back wall actually advertises the Grand Trunk Pacific Railroad of Canada! Readers might be forgiven for believing that there were no passengers using the room when the picture was taken, but a female passenger deep in her book can be seen reflected in the mirror.

Genuine Swiss
G.W.R.
GULF STREAM MYSTERY
WARM OCEAN CURRENT MAKES
CORNWALL
BRITAIN'S RIVIERA
THE GRAPHIC
THE WAR
BY OUR SPECIAL ARTIST
AEROPLANING IN MANY PHASES
GOOD-BYE TO COWES
The BYSTANDER
WHO, WHAT, & WHERE
A NEW SOCIAL FEATURE
COWES REGATTA
HOLIDAY PICTURES
2,000 Accident Assurance
LAND & WATER
QUEER STORIES
TRUTH
AUGUST MAGPIE
HANDY AIDS TO TRAVEL
GREAT WESTERN RAILWAY
Cornish Riviera
A TOUR IN GLORIOUS DEVON
FINANCIAL NEWS
THE KING'S SPEECH
DOMINION HOUSE
CONRAD'S FIRST PLAY
MEN & MORALITY
The Globe
THE PLUS MAN'S HANDICAP
THE DAMNS
BEST FOR
ENGLAND'S
8,000,000
HORSE SHOW
THE AWARDS
BIDEFORD REGATTA
INGERSOLL WATCHES
EAT EMPIRE FRUIT
FRUIT STORES LTD
OUR SPECIALITY
NESTLÉ'S
CHOCOLATE
GROWN IN SOUTH AFRICA

Above left Great Western publicity material is much in evidence in this view of the Wymans Bookstall at Paddington in August 1913. Two staff can faintly be seen in the dim interior, although it is some of the headlines recorded on the various posters that are of most interest. A wide variety of magazines are advertised, including *The Graphic*, which featured a 'Who, What & Where' feature in its edition of 16 August. A GWR poster boasts that the Gulf stream 'warm ocean current makes Cornwall Britain's Riviera'. Over 40 handbills advertise the company's 'Handy Aids to Travel' booklets priced at 2d each, while a poster advertising accelerated services to Cornwall is casually pinned to the end of the bookstall.

Left No fewer than three staff are shown in this 1927 picture of the Fruit Stores Ltd stall situated on platform 1. A dazzling selection of fruit is in evidence, including South African pineapples priced at 10d each; the wide choice available to GWR passengers may be explained by the fact that the picture was taken in the summer, although imported fruit is well to the fore, and a notice at the back of the stall urges travellers to 'give voluntary preference to fruit grown within the Empire, and to ask for same from the assistant'. In 1929 it was reported that the stall had won first prize in the grandly titled 'Empire Window Dressing Competition'. The cup, awarded by the Australian Government, was presented to the manageress by Sir James Milne, the GWR's General Manager, who also gave her a box of chocolates on behalf of the railway.

Above There are few passengers in evidence to take advantage of this much smaller confectionery stand situated between platforms 2 and 3. Teas, sweets and cigarettes are being sold, in addition to yet more fruit, which is again much in evidence in this 1923 view.

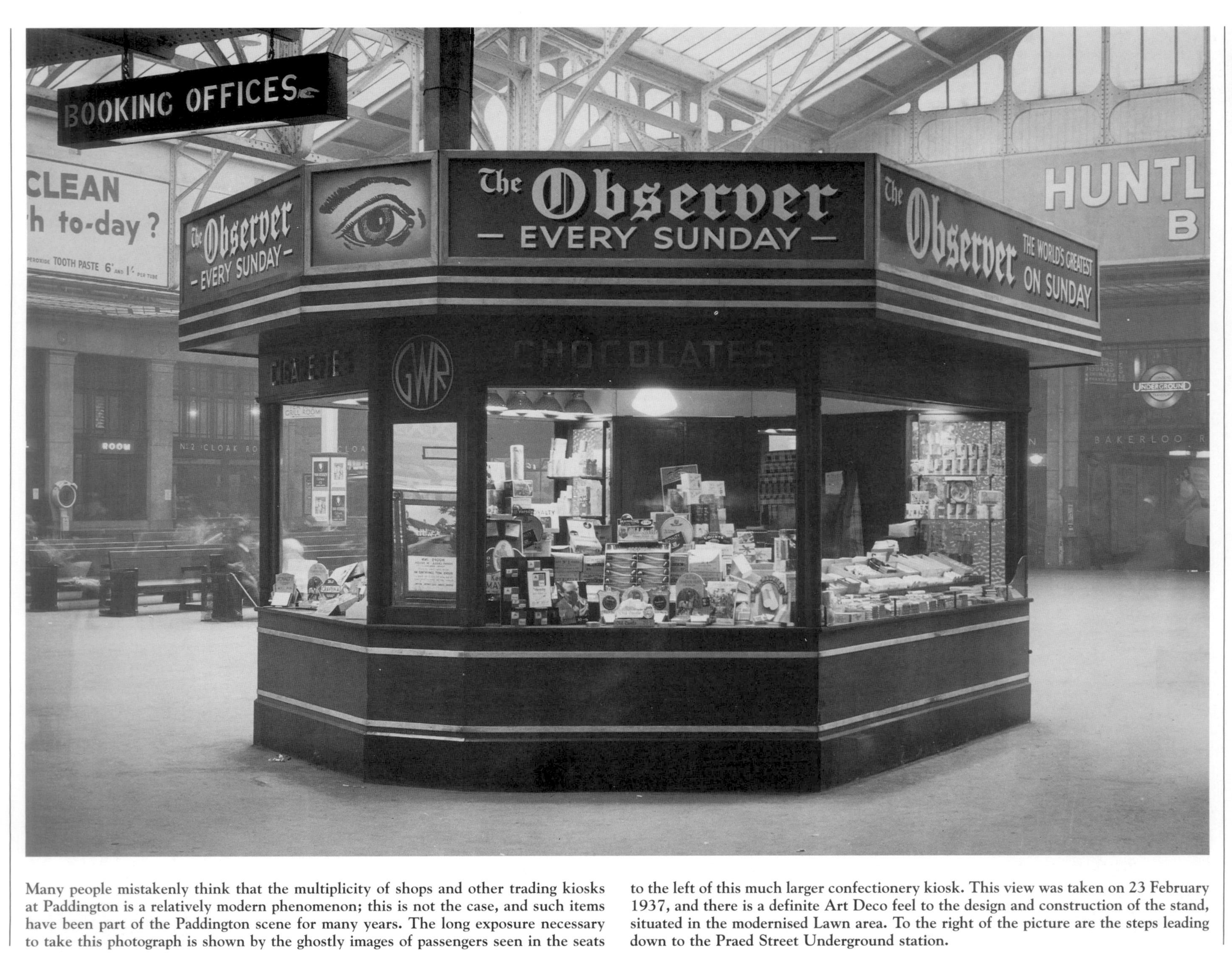

Many people mistakenly think that the multiplicity of shops and other trading kiosks at Paddington is a relatively modern phenomenon; this is not the case, and such items have been part of the Paddington scene for many years. The long exposure necessary to take this photograph is shown by the ghostly images of passengers seen in the seats to the left of this much larger confectionery kiosk. This view was taken on 23 February 1937, and there is a definite Art Deco feel to the design and construction of the stand, situated in the modernised Lawn area. To the right of the picture are the steps leading down to the Praed Street Underground station.

A tranquil scene within the Refreshment Rooms at Paddington around 1925 - presumably the public have been ushered out into the hustle and bustle of platform 1 while the picture was taken. However, it does give us a clearer view of the facilities provided for the Great Western traveller during this era. The marble pillars, rattan chairs and glass-topped tables lend an air of relaxed gentility, and on each table is a sugar bowl complete with silver tongs; these now fetch considerable amounts in auctions of railwayana, but then were merely commonplace. In 1937 a 'Quick lunch' and snack bar was opened on platform 1, where company publicity noted that customers could receive 'speedy and skilful service from white-coated chefs'. A menu of over 100 hot and cold items was provided, including soups, fish, poultry, salads, waffles and sandwiches 'cut in the presence of the customer'.

Above If passengers were not content with the facilities provided by the company in the form of the station refreshment rooms, they could also take advantage of the refreshment trolleys that plied their trade up and down the long platforms at Paddington. Dating from the First World War period, this picture was probably taken to illustrate not only the trolley but also the fact that it was being looked after by a woman. The company's name and initials are everywhere, not only on the china and the tea-cloth, but also embroidered into the attendant's hat. Considerable debate took place within the columns of the company's staff journal, the *Great Western Railway Magazine*, as to whether women should be allowed to do men's work, but the ever-growing demand for fit men for the forces meant that the employment of women became a necessity. Eventually over 25,000 company employees were to enlist in the forces during the course of the war.

Left This picture was taken in May 1937 and illustrates what must have been the final development of the refreshment trolley at Paddington. All manner of fare is available to the hungry traveller, including ham and beef sandwiches, sugared almonds, sticky buns and the ubiquitous fruit! The china shows the more modern 'shirt button' monogram design, as does the GWR 'Light Lunch Box' also featured at 1 shilling each. To the author's knowledge, none of these beautiful trolleys have survived, most probably being taken out of use in the austerity of the Second World War.

Right A wartime photograph of the refreshment trolley in action at Paddington; although its services seem to be appreciated by its customers, it is in rather less than pristine condition, compared to the one illustrated in the previous picture.

Below Another service provided for passengers at Paddington was the facility to be 'shaven, shorn and shampooed' in the Hairdressing Salon and baths, which were situated below ground level on platform 1. In a 1904 article the completion of these new facilities was described in some detail, since a fairly elaborate operation had been carried out in order to excavate under the platform for both this new service and new public lavatories. Next door to the salon seen here were hot and cold baths of which the weary traveller could make use. Four attendants were available to assist, and were, the article noted, being kept very busy.

Taxi!

Above The extensive taxi rank serving the station is situated between platforms 8 and 9. This photograph, taken on 5 September 1934, shows over 20 taxis waiting for business. There were normally around 40 parked inside the station, while the majority waited outside the train shed in a roadway that ran parallel to the station over the top of platforms 11 and 12. Such was the volume of business that the taxis were parked in four rows, with another row extending back into Praed Street. In the 1930s it was reported that on average 2,500 taxis passed through the station daily, with over a million fares being taken from Paddington in the course of a year. In the background a GWR Associated Daimler delivery lorry can just be seen at the foot of the ramp down which taxis are descending into the station itself. An oddity is the horse-drawn cab in the foreground, which seems rather at variance with its more modern counterparts parked nearby. A *GWR Magazine* article on the station noted that one customer who preferred horse power had kept a standing order for such a cab for over 37 years to meet him every Wednesday and Friday morning!

Left A rather different scene greets us some 27 years later in 1961. The cobbled roadway is gone, and the old taxis have been replaced by the more modern cabs still in use today, although older examples do feature in the distance. The London County Council ambulance is worthy of note, as is the mechanical tractor in the foreground used to transport parcels trolleys around the station. Taken from a position further down the station, there is an altogether more modern feel to the picture; once again a train has just arrived, although steam has now been replaced, and a Swindon-built diesel-hydraulic 'Warship' Class locomotive is seen at the head of modern British Railways-built Mark 1 carriages.

The Great Western Royal Hotel

The hotel at Paddington was designed not by Brunel, but by another Victorian architect, P. C. Hardwick; its construction coincided with the building of the new station, and it was opened by Prince Albert on 9 June 1854. The whole project was funded by an independent company that was associated with, but not run by, the Great Western; Brunel was for a time the Chairman of the Hotel board. In 1896 the operation was absorbed into the company's fledgling Hotels & Refreshment Room Department, which had begun the task of taking over facilities previously run by contractors; the year before it had bought back the contract for the infamous Swindon Refreshment Rooms.

The hotel had been open for almost 50 years by the time this photograph was taken in 1902, and the effects of smog and steam on the building are evident in the grimy exterior. A large porte-cochère was provided at the entrance to prevent guests from getting wet when leaving their carriages; also of note is the long line of GWR advertising posters visible on the railings leading to the departure road of the station on the left of the picture.

A rather different scene is presented in this view of the hotel taken in the late 1930s. Extensive modernisation took place in this period, coinciding with the more general improvements taking place in the station. As well as significant upgrading of the interior, substantial work was done to the outside of the building, as the photograph shows. Almost all the Victorian ironwork and decoration was stripped off, and the exterior now looks much more severe; the layers of grime have also been removed, improving its appearance immeasurably. The rise of the motor car is reflected in the removal of the old porte-cochère, and the filling in of the basement area in the front allowed a new entrance road to be created. On the extreme left of the picture is the last of the new office blocks built at Paddington; this building mirrored another new construction completed in 1933 on the arrival side. The completion of the office block next to the hotel filled a gap between the station and the hotel that can be seen clearly in the photograph of the departure road on page 15.

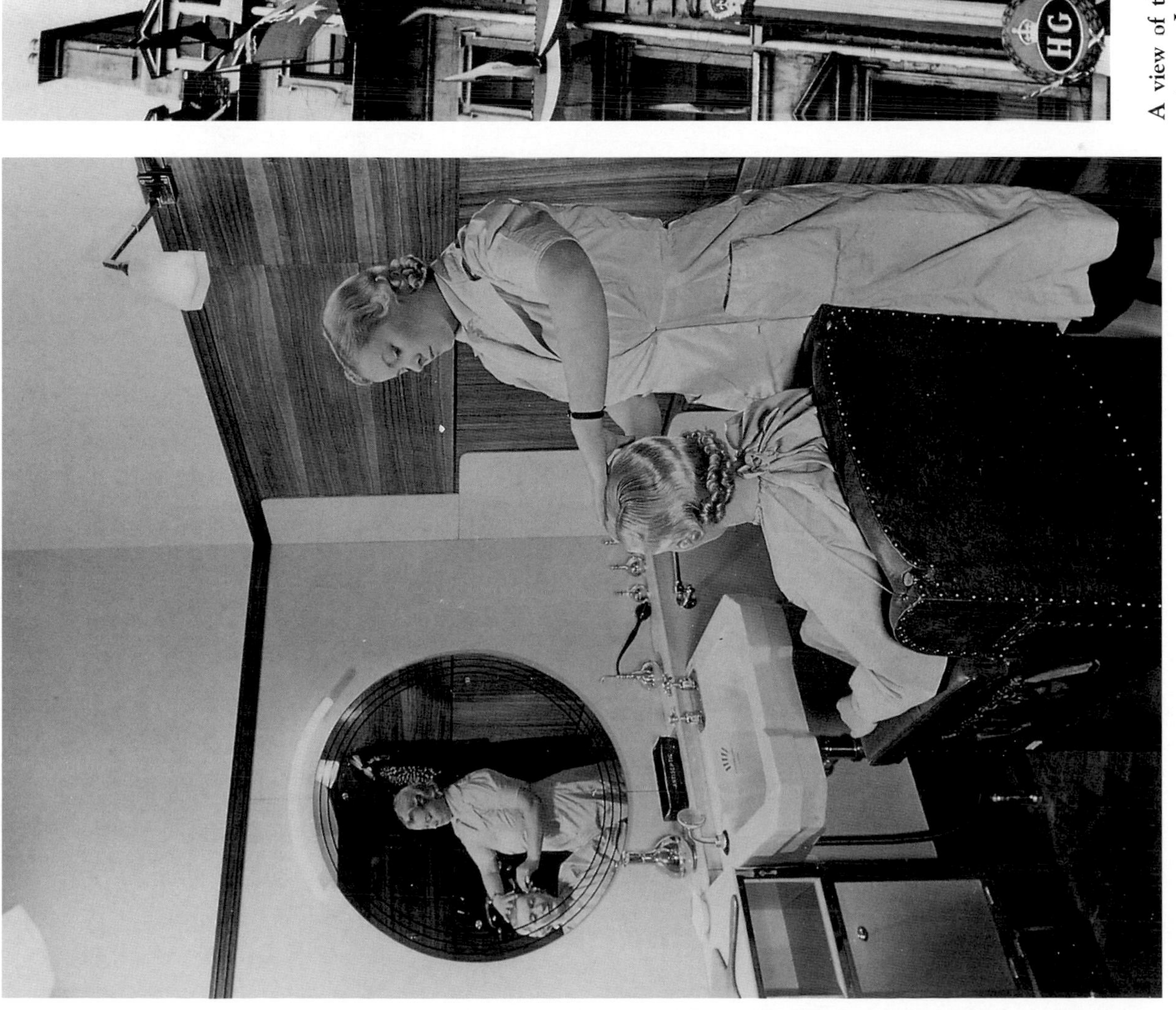

Right from its earliest days, the Great Western Royal Hotel was one of the best hotels in the capital, and residents had facilities of the highest quality. When it opened it had 165 rooms, and the standard of cuisine was second to none. One service provided for female guests was a hairdressing salon, and this view taken in the 1930s is so obviously posed that the two ladies in the picture could almost be twins! It is more likely that they are both members of staff; they certainly seem to have the same hairstyle!

A view of the front of the building, concentrating on the pediment over the main entrance. In his book on Great Western architecture, Adrian Vaughan describes the pediment as an allegorical sculpture describing 'Peace, Plenty and Industry'. By the time this photograph was taken, in 1946, the sculpture has once again succumbed to London dirt and grime, and it is the decorations occasioned by Victory celebrations that take the eye. As well as Britannia, the badges of the armed forces can be seen; the two shields marked 'HG' and 'CD' refer to 'Home Guard' and 'Civil Defence'. During the period of the celebrations in June 1946 the Royal Hotel was also floodlit.

2.
ARRIVALS AND DEPARTURES

Underground and suburban

Left One of the earliest developments at Paddington was the opening of the Metropolitan Railway in 1863, which was to link the station with the City of London some 4 miles away. Originally operated as a mixed gauge venture, the station at Paddington, which was known as Bishop's Road, was the terminus of the Metropolitan for a short while until the opening of the Hammersmith & City Railway (a joint venture between the GWR and the Metropolitan from 1867) a year later. Bishop's Road station was linked to the main terminus by a footbridge in 1870; it remained an important but separate part of station life until 1932 when it was extensively rebuilt to cope with increased suburban traffic. Two large island platforms were built, involving considerable construction work, and the station became part of Paddington proper, with the platforms not only serving Hammersmith & City electric services, but also Great Western suburban trains. Such was its integration that from 10 September 1933 it lost its separate name, and this 1950s view of platforms 14 and 15 shows the large nameboards clearly marked 'Paddington'.

Left A view of Paddington (Praed Street) station taken around 1910. Although opened in 1868, this station was on the Metropolitan line between Praed Street Junction and South Kensington and was not linked by subway to the Great Western terminus until 1887, before which passengers were forced to brave traffic and weather to reach it. The impressive overall roof was destroyed when the station received a direct hit in an air raid on 13 October 1940. GWR ARP staff played an important part in the rescue of passengers caught in the blast, although casualties were high. The roof has never been replaced, and the station is one of the busiest on the Circle Line today.

Waiting for the off

It is to be hoped that the reader will not be bored by the reproduction of a number of similar pictures locking over the main departure platforms, but careful scrutiny of the photographs reveals a wealth of detail recorded on the bulky plate cameras used by company photographers. This 1904 view records the scene before the departure of a West of England express. The last vehicle is one of the slip coaches used extensively by the Great Western, and the additional tail lamp required when coaches were slipped can be seen on the back of the next carriage. On the left of the picture two ladies are peering into a glass showcase occupied by the Railway Collecting Dog 'Tim'. He had been a familiar sight around the station, collecting money for charity; between 1892 and 1902, the year of his death, he collected over £800 for the GWR Widows & Orphans Fund. Something of a celebrity, when he did pass away he was stuffed, placed back on display and put back to work!

No4 PLATFOR
No2 PLATFORM No3
PLATFORM No1
TELEGRAPH OFFICE

Above Three locomotives are seen in this rather later view, which dates from just before the Great War. Although the negative is not of the best quality, there is still much to see. Three locomotives await the departure of the expresses, which will allow them to work back to Old Oak Common shed. Two of the engines are 'County' tanks; these short-lived engines spent most of their working lives in the London area, working fast and semi-fast passenger trains to Reading, Oxford and High Wycombe. Built between 1905 and 1912, the class was fairly short-lived by Great Western standards, and the construction of larger and more powerful '61xx' 2-6-2 tanks in the early 1930s led to their premature withdrawal. The engine on the far left, No 2243, was in fact the last of the class to be condemned, being taken out of service at the end of 1934. It was not actually cut up until 1939, surviving another five years for the heating of carriages at Old Oak Common. The other engine to be seen in this view is a 'Dean Goods', a humble 0-6-0 rarely seen in this grand location.

Left If the passengers in this photograph seem rather more well-heeled than those in previous views it is because they were awaiting a train to take them to a particularly grand occasion. The company photographer was called to record the departure of a number of special trains run for the annual Royal Garden Party at Windsor. The elegant lady in the foreground has her picnic basket near to hand, and the drab uniforms of the platform staff contrast strongly with the bonnets and straw boaters sported by the guests. In the background the delicate tracery of the decorative ironwork on the western screen of the train shed, which had been designed for Brunel by Matthew Digby Wyatt, can be seen.

The steam age

No. 73.

GREAT WESTERN RAILWAY.

PRIVATE AND NOT FOR PUBLICATION.

WORKING NOTICE OF

SPECIAL TRAINS

AND OTHER ARRANGEMENTS

IN CONNECTION WITH

HENLEY-ON-THAMES

ROYAL

REGATTA,

Wednesday, Thursday, Friday, and Saturday, July 1, 2, 3, & 4, 1914.

SPEED OF TRAINS—TWYFORD AND HENLEY.

Station.	From	To	Miles per hour.
Twyford ...	Down Main Line ...	Down Relief Line	25
,, ...	Down Relief Line ...	Henley Branch Line ...	10
,, ...	Henley Branch Line ...	Up Relief Line	10
,, ...	Up Relief Line	Up Main Line	25
Henley ...	Down Line	Nos. 1 & 2 Platforms & Bay	10

Explanation of General Notes in this Notice.

ML—Trains so marked run via Main Line.
RL—Trains so marked run via Relief Line.
Figures in small type (7 23), indicate the time at which a Train should pass a Station.
Light Engine.
† Empty Train.

(3000) Martin Billing, Son, and Co., Livery Street, Birmingham.

Left Cheap tickets were issued by the company on the occasion of this Henley Regatta in 1914; 1st Class returns cost 10 shillings and 2nd Class 6 shillings. The large numbers of passengers using the trains is illustrated by the fact that an additional 14 ticket collectors were employed at Paddington from 1 to 6 July, as well as another four booking clerks, who were to assist both in the main booking office and also two temporary offices situated on platforms 4 and 5.

Below left and below The lettering of this GWR timetable leaflet for 1912 has something of an 'Art Nouveau' feel to it, in contrast to the later example from 50 years later!

GREAT WESTERN

RAILWAY

TRAIN SERVICE

BETWEEN

LONDON

(PADDINGTON)

AND THE

PRINCIPAL STATIONS

ALSO

Through Cross Country Services,

AND

GENERAL INFORMATION.

PADDINGTON STATION,
February, 1912.

FRANK POTTER,
General Manager.

G.W.R.

WESTERN REGION

Principal Train Services

LONDON

(PADDINGTON)

and

SWINDON, CHIPPENHAM,

BATH, BRISTOL

and

WESTON-SUPER-MARE

18th JUNE to
9th SEPTEMBER inclusive,
1962

No. 120 BR35035/14

Printed in Great Britain by Joseph Wones, Ltd., West Bromwich

Above The pleasing lines of one of William Dean's beautiful 'Achilles' Class 4-2-2 locomotives can be seen in this undated picture taken just outside of the main train shed at Paddington; behind the engine the Digby Wyatt glass screens can again be clearly seen. In the era when this picture was taken locomotives were kept in absolutely spotless condition as this view shows, and it was reported that, once cleaned at the shed, the brass dome and other polished surfaces were often wrapped in sacking, not removed until the engine was coupled up to its train ready for departure. This locomotive, No 3050 *Royal Sovereign*, was built in February 1895, and had a very short life, being withdrawn in December 1915.

Below A superb postcard view of GWR 'Star' Class 4-6-0 No 4019 *Knight Templar* leaving Paddington on a West of England express just after the First World War. Built at Swindon in May 1908, this locomotive was one of the second batch of these powerful and well-loved locomotives designed by G. J. Churchward, and survived in traffic until October 1949. Before the more widespread introduction of 'Castle' Class locomotives in the mid-1920s, 'Stars' handled most of the fast services to the West Country. A varied selection of carriage stock can be seen behind the engine, most probably painted in the all-over chocolate livery adopted as an austerity measure in the Great War.

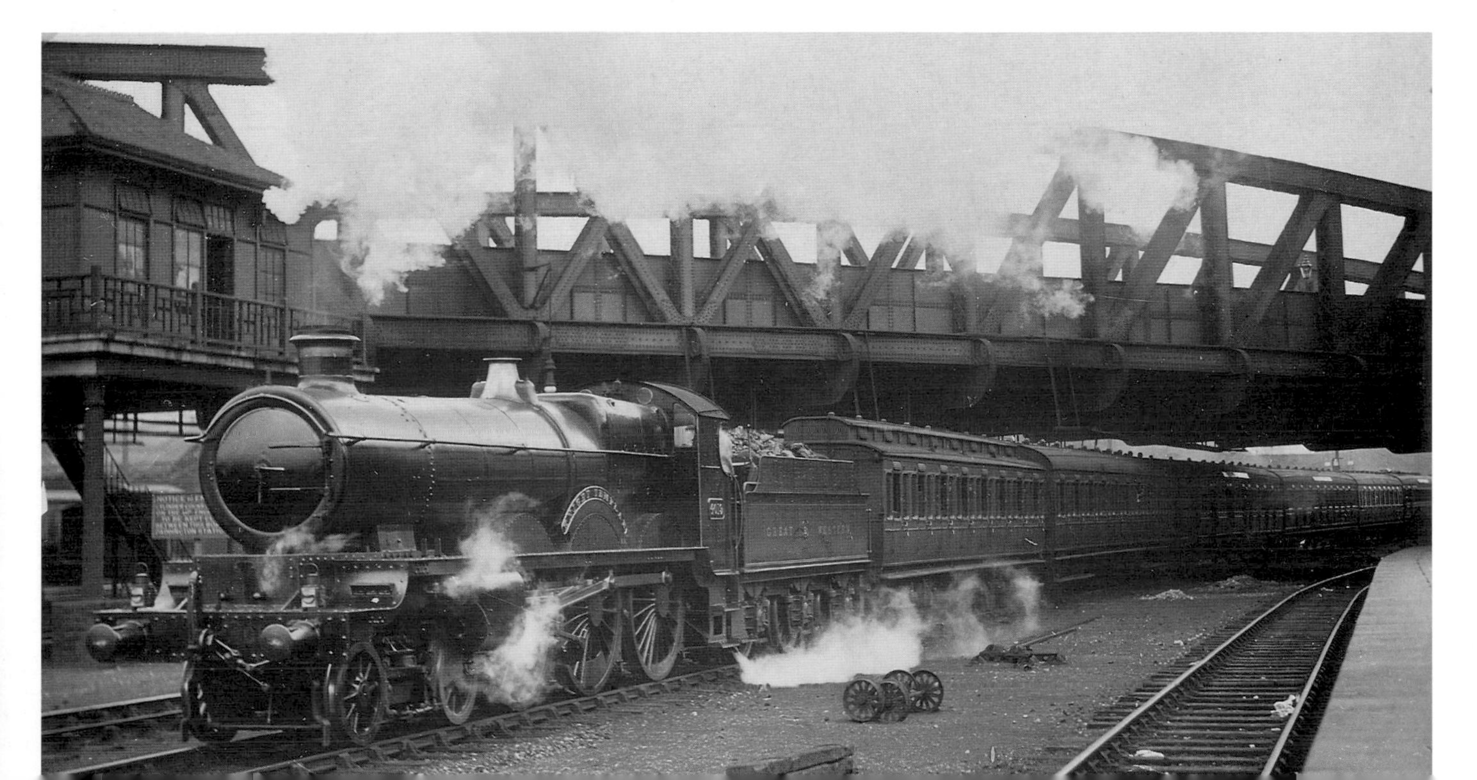

Above No date is given for this interesting photograph of one of the Great Western Railway's more unusual locomotives. The sun is glinting on the smokebox door of 4-4-2 No 104 *Alliance*, one of three compound locomotives purchased by the GWR from the French company Société Alsacienne des Constructions Mechaniques in the early years of the 20th century. It was the intention of G. J. Churchward to test them against his own 'Saint' and 'Star' designs, and although useful locomotives, it was decided to stick with the two- and four-cylinder system adopted by the GWR rather than the more complicated and expensive-to-maintain compound design. In later years the locomotives were heavily rebuilt at Swindon, and it is clear from this picture, taken some time before the withdrawal of No 104 in 1928, that it was certainly not the prettiest engine the company possessed!

Below The new and the old stand side by side on platform 2 at Paddington on 1 December 1933. The occasion was the press launch of a new diesel railcar built by the AEC company at Southall. The streamlined design of the vehicle contrasts starkly with the squat power of 4-6-0 No 6001 *King Edward VII*. The *GWR Magazine* described the railcar as looking 'not unlike a huge seaplane float'; some days later it was brought into regular service on stopping trains between Paddington and Didcot, with intermediate stops at Southall and Slough. Always popular with the travelling public, the company went on to acquire or build a further 37 examples of differing designs.

No clue to the identity of this locomotive is given by the photographer in this close-up view of the front end of an ex-GWR 'Castle' class engine as it waits to depart from platform 1. The 'Cheltenham Spa Express' was the successor to the 'Cheltenham Flyer', which was not reintroduced after the Second World War. The postwar version of the service left Paddington at 4.50 pm, and ran non-stop to Swindon rather than Kemble as the 'Cheltenham Flyer' had done. The construction of a new connection at Standish Junction on the old Midland main line between Bristol and Gloucester meant that trains from Swindon could run into Gloucester Eastgate station without reversing, arriving at 6.56 pm. The train finally terminated at Cheltenham at 7.16, at the old Midland station at Lansdown Road rather than the ex-Great Western terminal at St James's. Close examination of the locomotive shedplate shows that the engine was stabled at 85B, Gloucester, hardly surprising bearing in mind the service on which it was employed.

7007
BRITISH
RAILWAYS

4082

Left The 'Castle' Class locomotive seen in this photograph was built at Swindon in the final days of the Great Western Railway in July 1946 and was the last express engine to be built under GWR auspices. As a tribute to the company it was renamed *Great Western* in January 1948, carrying its original name, *Ogmore Castle*, for less than two years. Nameplates of this Class carrying non-standard names had the words 'Castle Class' added, and No 7007 also had the GWR coat of arms mounted on the splasher below.

Below left Departing on a westbound express on 28 August 1962 is another 'Castle', No 4082 *Windsor Castle*, looking rather less smart than it did when it hauled the funeral train of the late King George VI some 10 years before.

Above A fine broadside view of 'Castle' Class No 5017 *The Gloucestershire Regiment* outside the departure signal box at Paddington. The engine was originally built in 1932 as *St Donats Castle* and subsequently renamed after one of the most famous regiments in the Western Region area. One of the nameplates is now displayed at the Regimental Museum at Gloucester.

Right 'King' Class 4-6-0 No 6012 *King Edward VI* waiting to depart from Paddington on 4 August 1962. A month later the engine, built in April 1928, was withdrawn and stored at Wolverhampton (Stafford Road) shed, where it remained for a year before being cut up at the premises of Cox & Danks Ltd at Langley Green in October 1963.

Above During their last years in traffic the 'Kings' enjoyed something of a renaissance while running expresses between Paddington and Birmingham Snow Hill. However, the locomotives no longer received the level of cleaning and maintenance they had done previously. This undated view of No 6025 *King Henry III* arriving at Paddington shows the route destination crudely chalked on to the smokebox door, a far cry from the golden years of the Great Western.

Below Once out of the confines of the station trains could gain speed very quickly, and this superb photograph shows No 5019 *Treago Castle* accelerating away from Paddington on the 1.15 pm Paddington-Bristol service on 4 April 1957. Unlike sister engine No 7007 on page 38, this locomotive is fitted with the later flat-sided Hawksworth design of tender. The writers of the Great Western's 'Through the Window' series, which described the route from Paddington to various parts of the network, were singularly unimpressed with the sights to greet the traveller in the first few minutes of their journey. London had some pleasant suburbs, the guide noted, 'but it is too much to expect to see them from the train'. London, it continued, had the bad habit 'of showing her worst side to the railway'.

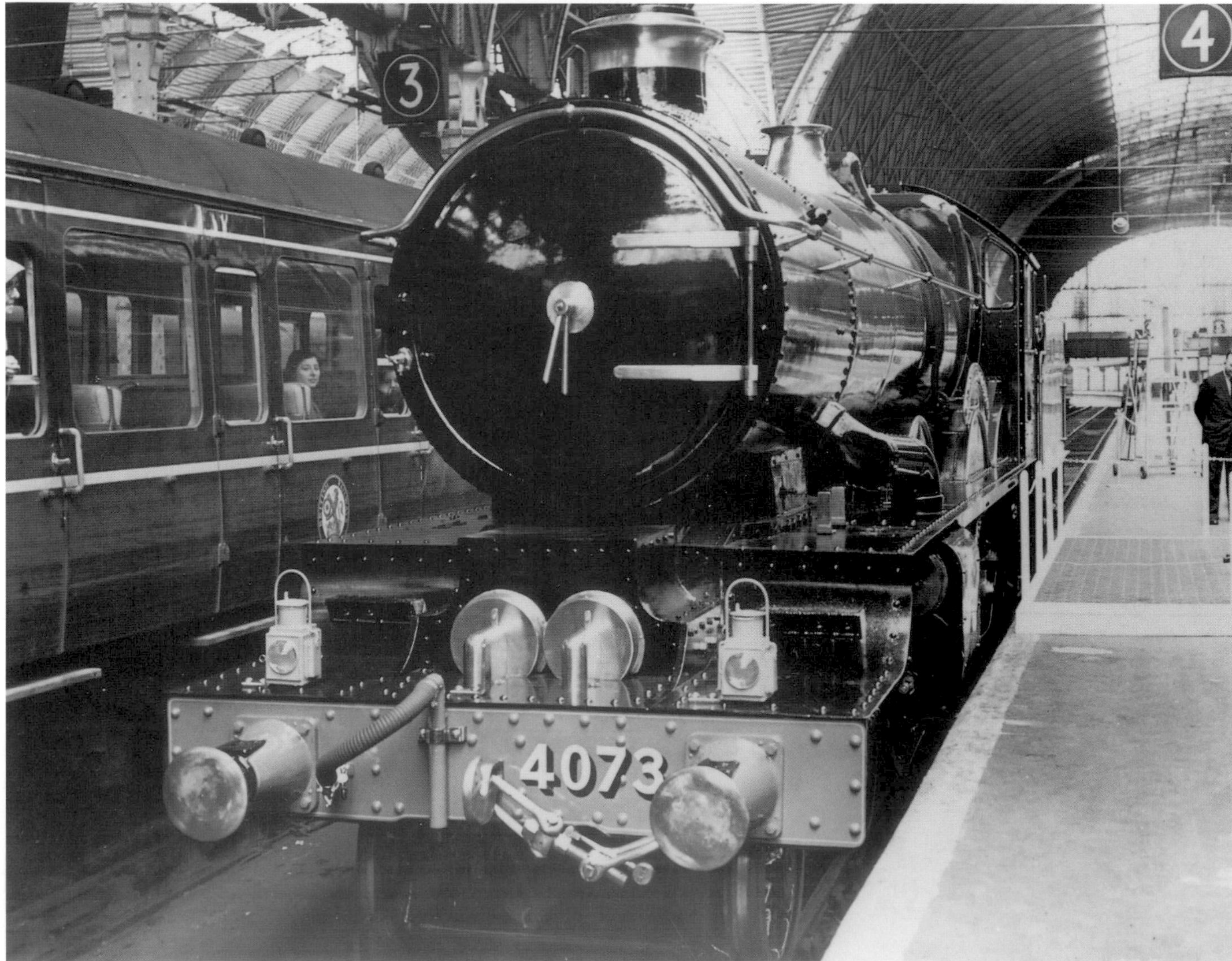
3
4
4073

Left The end of an era: Guard G. W. James checks the distinctive tail lamp of the last slip coach service to be run by British Railways on 9 September 1960. Slip coaches had been part of the Great Western scene from Broad Gauge days, and being able to 'slip' coaches at intermediate stations without stopping the train had allowed the GWR to run services like the 'Cornish Riviera Limited', which were non-stop yet provided for passengers wishing to alight at intermediate locations.

Below left Another indication of the end of the steam era. This photograph records the handing over of the first 'Castle' Class locomotive, No 4073 *Caerphilly Castle*, to the Science Museum at South Kensington in 1961. The engine was subsequently put on display at South Kensington, where it remained until 1996, when it was removed when the Land Transport gallery there was dismantled. At the time of writing it is on display at the Great Western Society's Didcot Railway Centre, pending a move to the new railway museum planned for Swindon. The highly polished condition of the engine, refurbished at Swindon during the last days of steam work there, contrasts strongly with some of the images of ex-Great Western locomotives featured in previous photographs.

Tank locomotives

Above and right Although Paddington has been the backdrop for many photographs of some of the finest and most powerful express locomotives produced by the Great Western, it was also the preserve of countless smaller tank locomotives, which fussed busily around the terminus for most of its history. Since there were no 'run-round' facilities at Paddington, station pilot engines were needed to bring in and take out rolling-stock to and from the carriage sidings at Old Oak Common. The 'Up and Down' link, as it was known, consisted latterly of pannier tank locomotives, predominantly '57xx' types; these two photographs feature two such examples of the class, Nos 5744 and 5732, built within months of each other in 1929.

Above After the Second World War, pilot work was also tackled by examples of F. W. Hawksworth's '9400' Class. Built using more modern techniques, these rather ugly-looking locomotives were intended to replace some of the older panniers. No date is given for this picture of No 9479 working empty stock into Paddington.

Below F. W. Hawksworth's similarly rather ungainly '1500' Class 0-6-0 pannier tanks were built at Swindon after nationalisation in June 1949. Constructed with austerity in mind, the class featured much welded fabrication, and outside valve gear, quite unlike anything seen on the Great Western, was adopted for ease of maintenance. No 1505 simmers under the great roof at Paddington in 1955.

Above and right Tank locomotives were also extensively used on London suburban services, and in the late 1920s the 'County' tanks (illustrated on page 32) and 2-4-0 'Metro' tanks like those illustrated here dominated these duties. The superb overhead view of No 3583 was taken at the buffer stops at Paddington; there appears to be little coal left in the bunker, and the fireman's coal-pick is perched next to one of the rear cab windows.

The second photograph shows No 3596 bringing a train into Paddington, with the Goods Depot in the background. Although no date is given for the photographs, they probably date from the 1920s. Both engines were built in 1899, and both survived in traffic until the 1940s. Some of the class were fitted with condensing apparatus, which allowed them to work through the underground lines of the Metropolitan.

Below One of C. B. Collett's '61xx' Prairie tank locomotives, No 6144, built at Swindon in 1932, is seen on pilot duty at Paddington in June 1959. Although built for London suburban traffic, the influx of diesel multiple units (DMUs) to this traffic in the late 1950s meant that they were relegated to more humble duties, hence the appearance of this larger locomotive on pilot work.

Ranelagh Bridge

Above When Old Oak Common Depot opened in 1906, the old locomotive sheds at Westbourne Park were demolished. Since Old Oak was some considerable distance away from the terminus, there was still a need for a turntable close to the station, to allow locomotives from other sheds to be turned, coaled and watered quickly ready for their return journey. The small depot at Ranelagh Bridge, an outstation of Old Oak Common, was opened in 1908, and had minimal facilities. In this photograph 'King' Class 4-6-0 No 6006 *King George I* is being turned on the 65-foot turntable on 30 March 1957.

Left As this photograph shows, Ranelagh Bridge backed closely on to a row of houses, and conditions for local residents could have hardly been ideal. Over the years both Great Western and British Railways management received a string of complaints from local people. The end of steam did not make matters any better, since if anything diesel locomotives were noisier, and with their engines running for long periods of time, it must have been very unpleasant, particularly at night. One such locomotive, the prototype Brush *Falcon* locomotive, is seen at the depot on 9 September 1971.

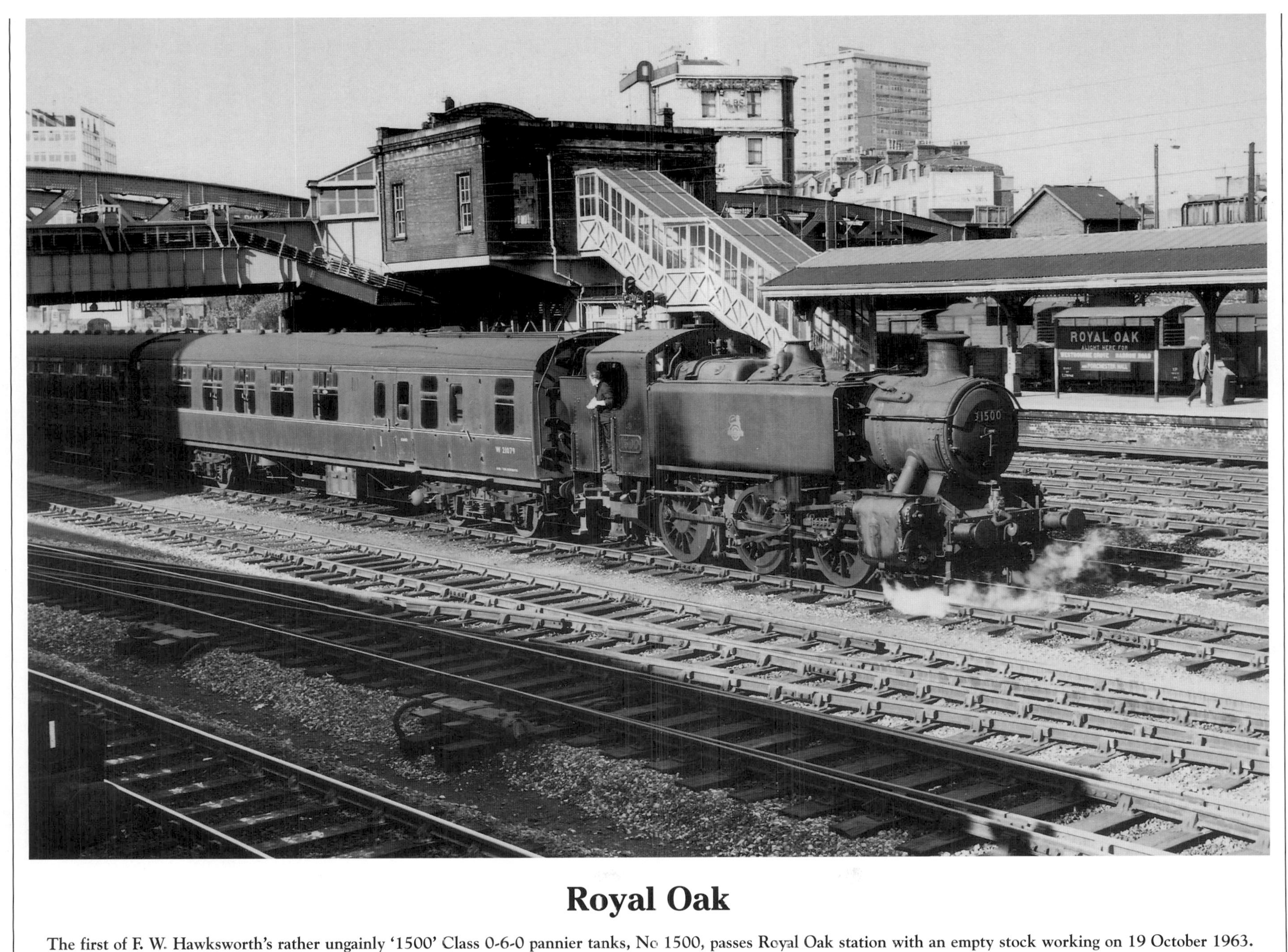

Royal Oak

The first of F. W. Hawksworth's rather ungainly '1500' Class 0-6-0 pannier tanks, No 1500, passes Royal Oak station with an empty stock working on 19 October 1963. The booking office for the Hammersmith & City station was situated on the bridge carrying Porchester Road, and the notice hanging below the Royal Oak station sign reads 'Alight here for Westbourne Grove, Harrow Road and Porchester Hall'.

Below A shovel rests against a platform chocolate machine on Royal Oak station as workmen struggle to clear the wreckage caused by an air raid on the night of 6 November 1940. It is not recorded if there were any casualties on the badly damaged coach.

Bottom Over the bridge from Royal Oak station was the Great Western Railway's stationery store in Porchester Road. Built in 1905, this building housed much of the company's spare or used paperwork. In an enterprise as large as the Great Western, which relied heavily on bureaucracy, the amount of paper generated was tremendous; the catalogue issued by the GWR of its paperwork runs to many pages, and includes forms for almost every aspect of the railway's operation, from staff matters to materials ordering procedures. In later years this building was the repository for Great Western archive material before it was transferred to the Public Record Office at Kew. The most interesting aspect of this photograph, taken not long after the store opened, is that the photographer appears to have arrived in time to witness a motor accident on Porchester Road. There is a large crowd around two vehicles, one of which appears to have mounted the pavement. At this period cars would still have been something of a novelty, and even passengers on the bus crossing the bridge are craning their necks to see what has happened!

3.
MOVING THE GOODS

Milk, mail and parcels

Like all the main stations in the capital, Paddington played a vital role in the handling of milk traffic in and out of London. Thousands of gallons of fresh milk were needed by thirsty Londoners, and until the station had been modernised, traffic was dealt with on a fairly haphazard basis. To give an idea of the scale of the problem, in the 1920s Paddington was handling around 5,500 full churns of milk each day; and a similar number had to be removed and returned to their station of origin! This scene on platform 1, taken just before the Great War, illustrates how much space the large number of milk churns handled by the GWR took up on the crowded platforms at Paddington. Porters and station staff needed to be fit and strong to lift the churns, which were awkward when empty, but even worse when full of milk.

Above The difficulties involved in the handling of milk churns were to a great extent removed with the construction of new facilities in the early part of the First World War, when the new roof span was added (see pages 81 and 82). As part of the project, a new platform, No 12, was built to handle milk and to a lesser extent fish and parcels traffic. At the back of the platform, as can be seen in this view, a sunken road was built, which allowed up to 20 milk floats to be loaded without lifting being required. In its account of the work done, the company magazine noted that the 750-foot platform varied in height from 3 feet at the Bishop's Road end (suitable for passenger traffic), to 3 ft 9 in for the milk section, allowing churns to be rolled straight out of wagons. Access to the platform was from a new ramp up to London Street, and the floor was, the magazine continued, paved with 'hit and miss' material so as to give horses a good foothold. Unlike the rest of the station, run-round facilities were provided in the form of a 'scissors' crossover. This atmospheric picture, reproduced in the *GWR Magazine* article, shows that construction is far from complete, with heavy girders, possibly from the cab road bridge, still lying ready for erection.

Below A milk train stands at the new platform at Paddington in July 1923. Behind the locomotive is a very varied selection of rolling-stock, most being six-wheeled examples of the 'Siphon' milk wagon used extensively by the Great Western to transport milk in 17-gallon churns. Since there was no refrigeration at this period, the wagons had large slatted sides, which allowed air to circulate freely around the churns, keeping the milk relatively cool. In later years the company built larger bogie versions of these vehicles, which were used extensively before the move to the bulk carrying of milk led to the introduction of tanker wagons. The locomotive is unusual, being 4-4-0 No 4119, a member of the 'Badminton' Class built at Swindon in 1899; when this picture was taken it had only another six years of service left.

An early photograph of the scene on platform 8, taken in 1905 before the extensive modernisation of the station that took place from 1913 onwards. Barriers have been drawn across the platform to keep the public away from the unloading of mail from the United States, which has been brought up to the capital by an Ocean Mail Special from Plymouth. Horse-drawn Royal Mail wagons are waiting to speed the letters away, and sacks marked 'US Mail' still lie on the platform. Large transatlantic liners anchored off the Great Western's port at Plymouth and the mail was loaded on to small tenders, which brought it to Plymouth Millbay station where it was reloaded on to special trains bound for Paddington. The Great Western competed fiercely with the London & South Western Railway for this traffic, and it was on one of these specials in 1906 that the GWR engine No 3440 *City of Truro* became the first steam locomotive to break the 100 mph barrier. Note in the middle of the platform a bowler-hatted official checking that all is well.

Until relatively recently Paddington, like many other major stations, had another life, largely unseen by the public, when in the small hours staff loaded and unloaded mail, parcels and other commodities. With the opening of a centralised Royal Mail depot at Willesden in 1996, the use of Paddington by the Royal Mail ceased entirely, while road traffic has taken much other business away from railways, including some newspaper traffic. This evocative photograph shows the loading of newspapers on platform 4 in the 1930s. The development of what we would now call the popular press was revolutionised by railways since newspapers could be printed and distributed very quickly to even the farthest parts of the country. Newspaper proprietors like Alfred Harmsworth, the founder of the *Daily Mail*, could boast that their titles were on sale simultaneously everywhere, something that had not been possible before the coming of the railway.

Little attention has yet been paid as to how the goods and other commodities described so far were moved around the confines of the station itself. Mechanical tractors were used to haul luggage trolleys around, but much work still relied on staff muscle power. This picture, taken on platform 1 in 1942 during the Second World War, shows a female member of staff hauling a motley selection of parcels and other goods on a station hand trolley.

Another wartime photograph featuring women porters unloading a GWR horse-drawn dray, stacked high with all manner of suitcases and packages. Many passengers took advantage of the PLA scheme (Passenger Luggage in Advance), which allowed them to send heavy cases and bags ahead in advance of their journey. In crowded trains this was a distinct advantage, although sometimes cases could go astray!

The Goods Department

Built on the site of the old 1838 passenger station, the Paddington Goods Department was an enormous undertaking, similar though not equal in size to its nearby passenger counterpart. By 1932 it employed 1,950 staff, a number that had remained fairly constant since the turn of the century. Considerable rebuilding work was necessary after a disastrous fire in 1896; the capacity of the depot was increased by another 60 wagons by the lengthening of platforms, shunting horses were replaced by hydraulic capstans, and new offices were also built. The latter can be seen to the right of the Red Lion public house in this turn-of-the-century view. The Goods Depot is beyond the bridge, while wagons awaiting loading or dispatch wait in sidings; a shunting locomotive can be seen waiting for duty in the distance. The quality of the picture reveals much detail for the railway historian or modeller, from the gleaming brass on the dome of the shunting locomotive on the right, to the chalked destinations on the wagons waiting in the sidings. The electrified lines of the Hammersmith & City Railway can also be seen in the centre of the picture.

The massive retaining wall of the Goods Depot provided a familiar backdrop for many hundreds of photographs of trains coming in and out of Paddington; this facade dated from further rebuilding of the depot that took place in the 1920s. In this view 'Castle' Class 4-6-0 No 7018 *Drysllwyn Castle* is dwarfed by the rather unsightly retaining wall as it brings the 11.45 Bristol-Paddington service into the station on 15 June 1965. It should also be mentioned at this point that Paddington as not the only major goods facility that the Great Western had in the capital; a large depot was opened in South London at South Lambeth in 1913, and there were also depots at Poplar and Victoria & Albert Docks. Great Western goods trains also ran through the Metropolitan underground lines to Smithfield Market in the heart of the City of London where they also had a substantial goods station.

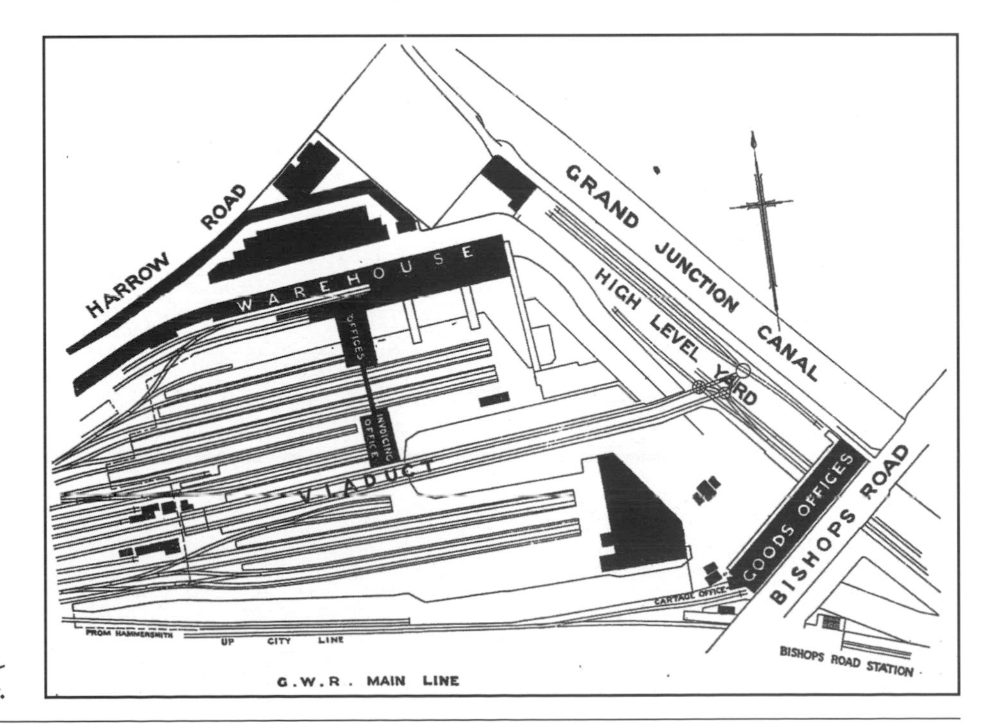

A plan of the Goods Depot before modernisation in the early part of the 20th century.

The interior of the Goods Depot in 1942. This particular picture was taken to illustrate the arrival of one of the Great Western's best-known special goods traffic, broccoli. The vegetable was moved from Cornwall to the capital in special high-speed trains, allowing Londoners to obtain fresh produce very quickly. A large number of staff have assembled for the photograph, a high proportion of whom are women.

In general, the Goods Depot was organised so that between noon and midnight, the majority of traffic bound for other parts of the Great Western was sorted, checked and loaded into the correct wagons, and the period between midnight and noon saw the reverse of this process, with goods bound for London, like this broccoli, being sorted and loaded ready for distribution.

Distribution of goods from the depot was of paramount importance; it was imperative that goods, especially fresh items such as fruit and vegetables, were delivered as quickly as possible, and the Great Western had an enormous fleet for vehicles to perform this task. 'Here today and there tomorrow' was one of the phrases used by the company in its publicity. Some measure of the scale of the fleet in the days when horse-drawn vehicles dominated can be seen in this picture taken at Paddington during the General Strike, when virtually all vehicles were confined to the depot itself.

As was typical, the company issued a special rule book or 'Cartage Instruction Book', giving staff detailed instructions on how to look after both their vehicles and their horses. 'Teasing of horses is forbidden,' it warns, 'since it tends to make them vicious.' Although by 1939 motor vehicles had taken over much of the work done by horses, the company still saw fit to reissue the rules, with an appendix on what to do in an air raid. In such an event, staff were instructed to tie the horse to the rear of the vehicle, with its nose-bag on!

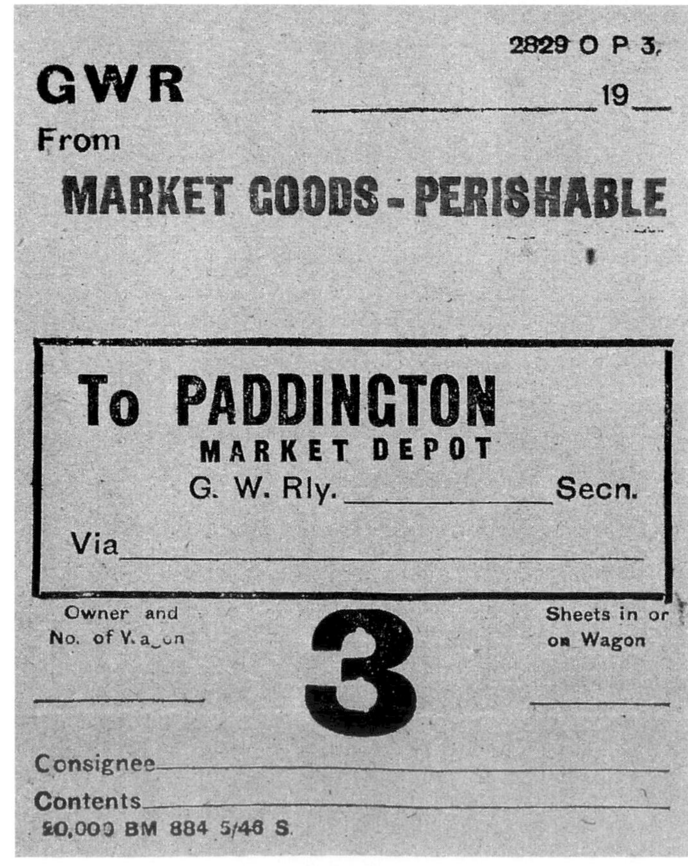

2829 O P 3.

GWR ______________ 19__

From

MARKET GOODS - PERISHABLE

To PADDINGTON

MARKET DEPOT

G. W. Rly. ______________ Secn.

Via ______________

Owner and No. of Wagon ______ **3** Sheets in or on Wagon ______

Consignee ______________

Contents ______________

20,000 BM 884 5/46 S.

Above As can be seen from this view of the back of the Goods Depot, taken on 12 November 1940, the yard backed on to the canal, and the purpose of the picture was to show the effects of a minor air raid, which had caused an LMS delivery wagon to be blown into the canal, where it can be seen sticking forlornly out of the water. There was access from the canal into the depot for loading and unloading, but this was little used in later years. In an instruction book relating to London Goods Traffic issued to staff at country stations in 1924, it was noted that 'Traffic to or from barges on the Grand Junction Canal can be transferred from or to Railway Wagons, but before accepting such traffic . . . the agent must be communicated with in order that arrangements may be made for delivery to barge.'

Left A GWR wagon label from about 1946.

4.
COMPANY SERVANTS

Paddington staff

Throughout this volume much is described about the changes in the station structure and fabric, the trains services and the locomotives and rolling-stock used. It should not, however, be forgotten that without the staff to operate the station, none of the former would be of great importance. In 1933 it was recorded that the passenger station employed 1,389 staff of all grades. Amongst this enormous total were porters, guards, shunters, ticket collectors, clerks, refreshment room staff and a whole range of other miscellaneous people who all contributed to the running of this vast enterprise.

Amongst all these staff one of the more lonely tasks was that of the station announcer, and this photograph is included, even though it has been reproduced before, to illustrate one of the more unusual tasks. A loudspeaker system was only introduced in the early 1930s as part of the more general improvements made when the Lawn was refurbished. It was reported that there were teething problems with the system, and additional loudspeakers had to be installed to enable passengers to hear the announcements clearly.

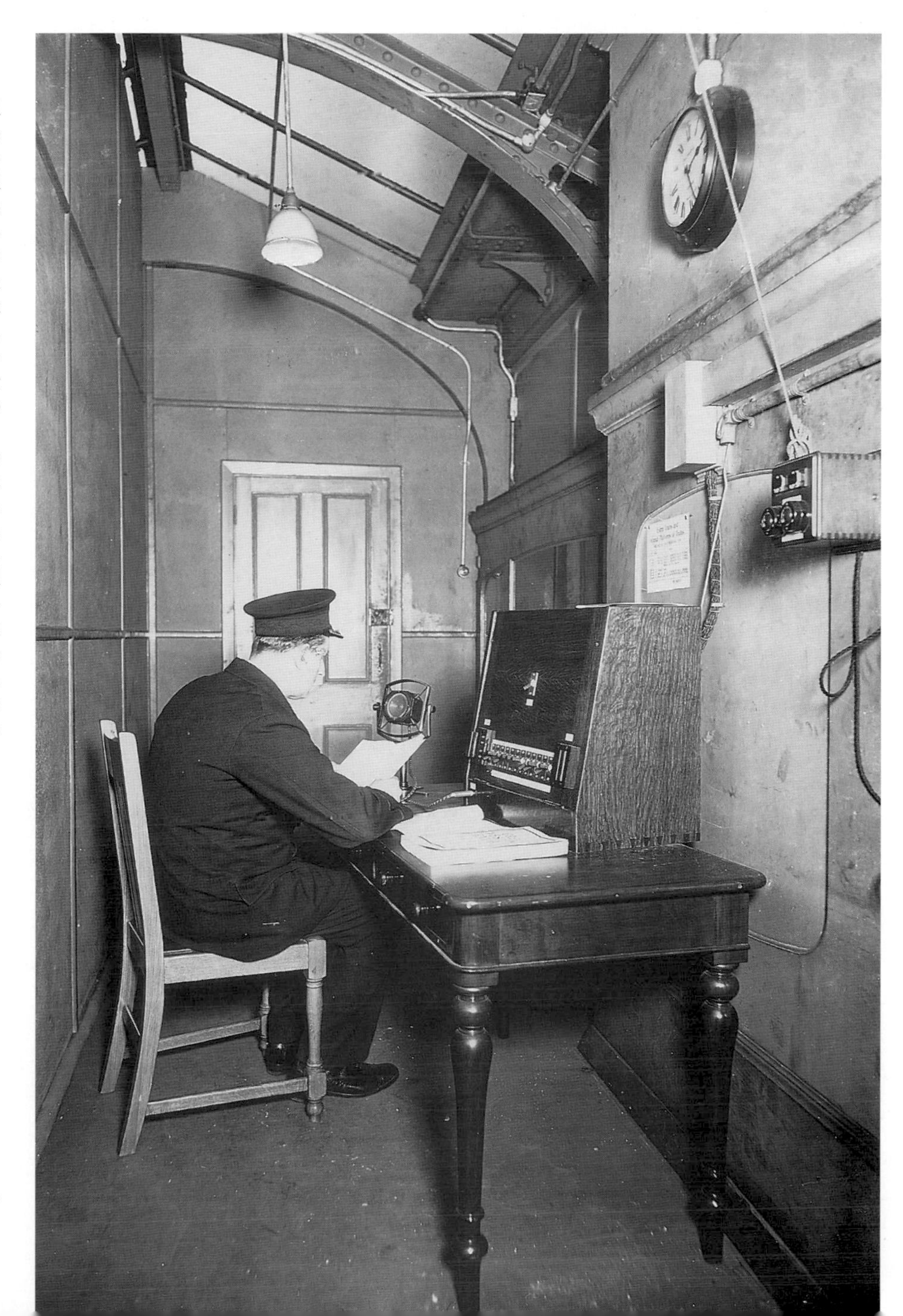

This view of a ticket collector at work probably dates from the Second World War, since the passenger at the rear wearing spectacles appears to have a gas mask case slung over his shoulder. The man having his ticket checked looks every inch the 'City gent' with his bowler hat and rolled umbrella. After some considerable time as an 'open' station where tickets were only checked by staff on trains, ticket checks were reintroduced at Paddington on 16 November 1996. Another Great Western peculiarity can be seen in the spelling of the notice to the right of the entrance to the platform, which reads 'Season tickets must be *shewn* here'.

The luggage piled high on the first trolley hauled by this 'mechanical horse' seems to be perilously balanced in this 1942 view of two female station staff on platform 6 at Paddington. A number of the loudspeakers for the public address system can be seen suspended by cables above the carriages in the background.

No doubt the Health & Safety Executive would have something to say about the safety precautions taken by the company in order to allow staff to clean the walls around and above the Directors balcony on platform 1. However, the two ladies balancing on the planks, which are rather haphazardly suspended between the balcony itself and a very tall set of steps, do not seem unduly concerned. It is very easy to see how much progress the cleaners have made in this April 1942 view, and the picture clearly illustrates how dirty the terminus became through constant exposure to the soot, dirt and smoke given off by steam locomotives.

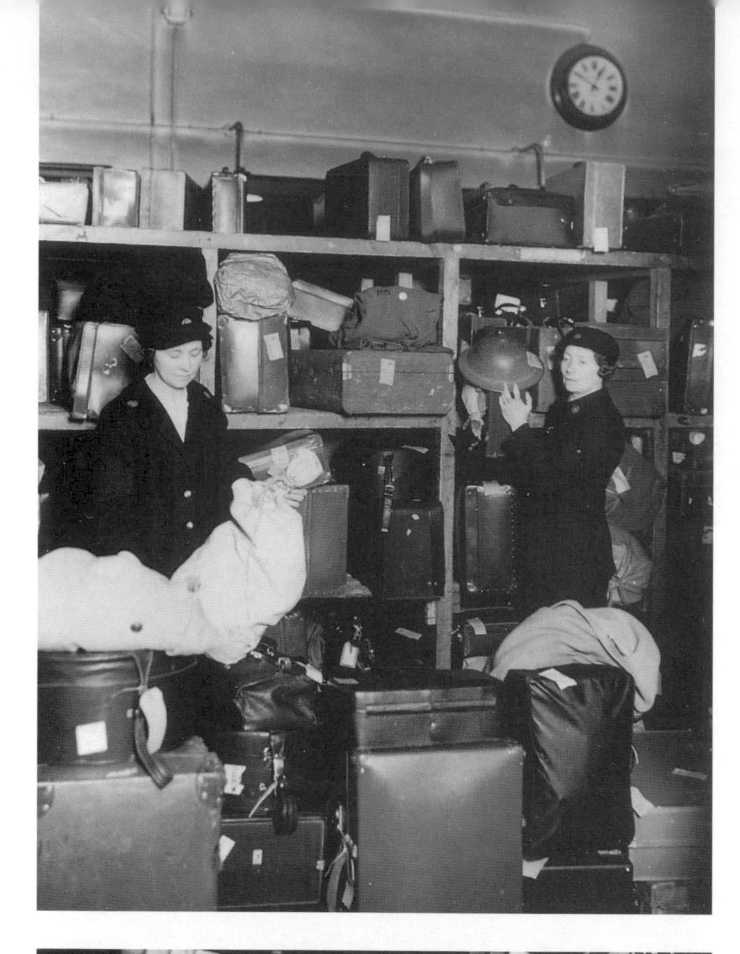

Left A further wartime photograph of staff at work in the Left Luggage department, which was situated on platform 1 near the Lawn. Always a busy part of the station, the pressures brought to bear by the large number of people travelling during the war period are obvious. Many servicemen breaking their journey while on leave needed to deposit some of their bulkier kit, and the porter on the right of the picture has a combat helmet in her hand.

Below left An important task, especially for such a publicity conscious company as the Great Western, was the checking and fixing of posters at various sites in and around the station. This 1942 photograph shows a member of staff pasting a large and at that time particularly relevant poster urging the public to mark Remembrance Day by wearing a poppy. The large ladder is clearly marked 'GWR Commercial Advertising Department'.

Below The final picture in this sequence from 1942 is of another ticket inspector, this time recorded checking a passenger's ticket actually on the train. In the background the dials of the clock on platform 1 can just be seen.

Right Staff at Paddington had a range of social facilities available to them, as this advertising card shows. There was an extensive library available through the Literary Society, as well as many other sporting and recreational clubs and societies. Staff could also join the 'Great Western Dining Club', which had been established as early as 1859. The object of this society was, its rules noted, 'to provide its members with food and refreshment including excisable liquor . . . and to arrange for proper recreation and entertainment for them'.

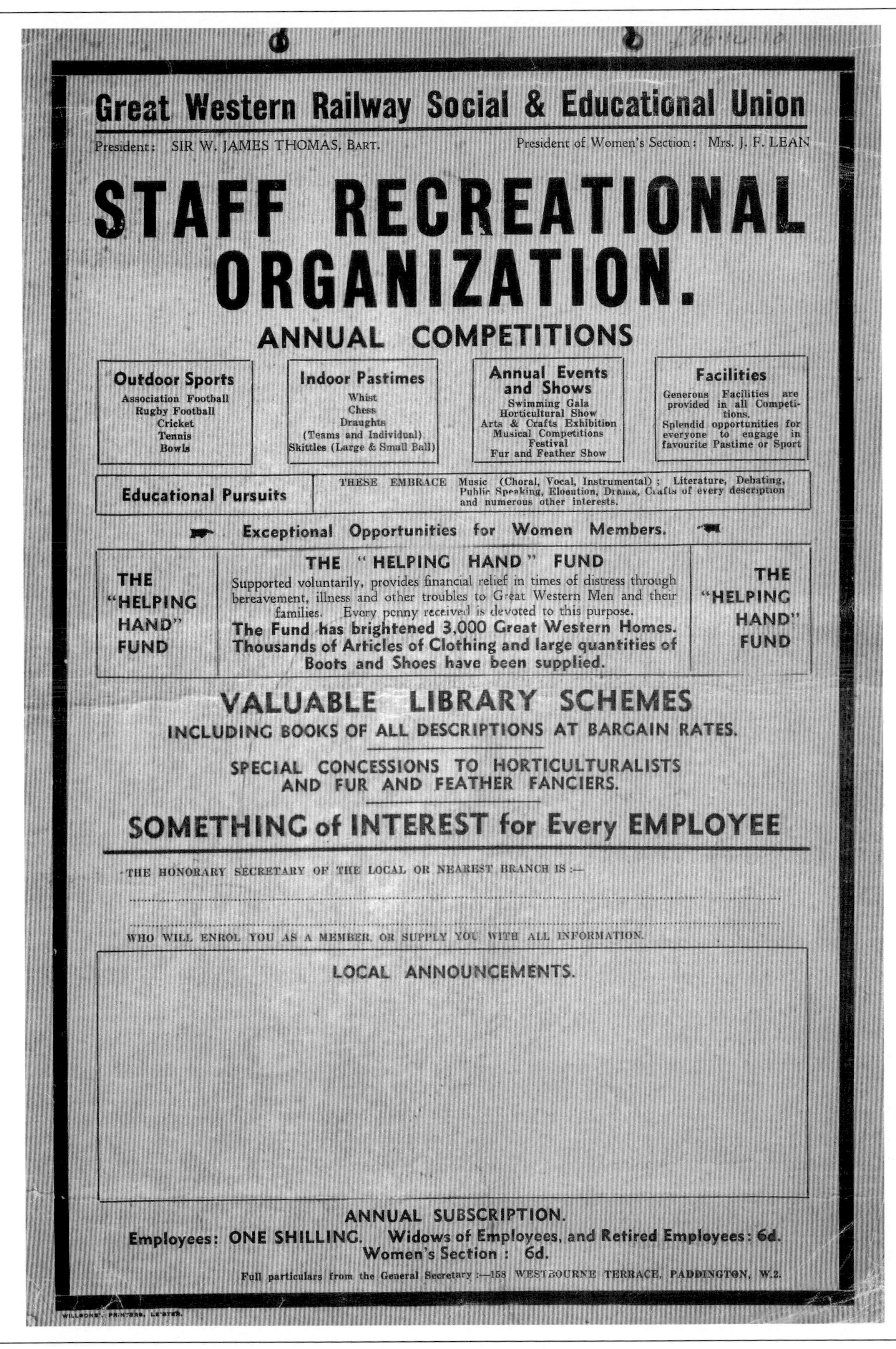

Great Western Railway Social & Educational Union

President: SIR W. JAMES THOMAS, BART. President of Women's Section: Mrs. J. F. LEAN

STAFF RECREATIONAL ORGANIZATION.

ANNUAL COMPETITIONS

Outdoor Sports	Indoor Pastimes	Annual Events and Shows	Facilities
Association Football Rugby Football Cricket Tennis Bowls	Whist Chess Draughts (Teams and Individual) Skittles (Large & Small Ball)	Swimming Gala Horticultural Show Arts & Crafts Exhibition Musical Competitions Festival Fur and Feather Show	Generous Facilities are provided in all Competitions. Splendid opportunities for everyone to engage in favourite Pastime or Sport

Educational Pursuits — THESE EMBRACE Music (Choral, Vocal, Instrumental); Literature, Debating, Public Speaking, Elocution, Drama, Crafts of every description and numerous other interests.

Exceptional Opportunities for Women Members.

THE "HELPING HAND" FUND

THE "HELPING HAND" FUND

Supported voluntarily, provides financial relief in times of distress through bereavement, illness and other troubles to Great Western Men and their families. Every penny received is devoted to this purpose.

The Fund has brightened 3,000 Great Western Homes. Thousands of Articles of Clothing and large quantities of Boots and Shoes have been supplied.

THE "HELPING HAND" FUND

VALUABLE LIBRARY SCHEMES

INCLUDING BOOKS OF ALL DESCRIPTIONS AT BARGAIN RATES.

SPECIAL CONCESSIONS TO HORTICULTURALISTS AND FUR AND FEATHER FANCIERS.

SOMETHING of INTEREST for Every EMPLOYEE

THE HONORARY SECRETARY OF THE LOCAL OR NEAREST BRANCH IS:—

....

WHO WILL ENROL YOU AS A MEMBER, OR SUPPLY YOU WITH ALL INFORMATION.

LOCAL ANNOUNCEMENTS.

ANNUAL SUBSCRIPTION.

Employees: ONE SHILLING. Widows of Employees, and Retired Employees: 6d.

Women's Section: 6d.

Full particulars from the General Secretary:—158 WESTBOURNE TERRACE, PADDINGTON, W.2.

Station offices

As well as being the largest and most important station on the Great Western, Paddington was also the administrative headquarters of the company. In the earliest days of the railway, board meetings had been held at both Bristol and London, and also for a short time at Steventon in Oxfordshire. The construction of Brunel's great terminus meant that a board room of some importance could be constructed, and this was done on the first floor overlooking platform 1. This picture was taken in 1905, and a plan of Fishguard Harbour can be seen on the back wall, next to the enormous plan of the GWR and its connections. Over the mantlepiece hangs a portrait of Sir Daniel Gooch, the company's first Locomotive Engineer, who became Chairman in 1865.

A scene of devastation on 17 April 1941. The effects of the parachute mine that dropped on the departure side of the station have already been described, and this photograph shows the board room wrecked by debris that has dropped from the floor above. The clock seen on the mantelpiece in the previous picture is amazingly unscathed, as is the glass-fronted bookcase next to the door. The board room table itself is buried under a huge pile of plaster and other material. Above, a desk is perched precariously above a gaping hole in the side of the building.

More evidence of the damage done to the offices at Paddington in the April 1941 raid. This was the scene on what was known as the third corridor in the same block as the board room. It was fortunate that the company had carried out an evacuation of its own staff in 1939, moving most of its administrative staff to Berkshire where most Great Western business continued in special facilities built for the staff at Aldermaston; six steel-framed brick-built buildings housed offices for most departments, although use was also made of large houses in the vicinity such as Crookham House and Beenham Grange.

The board room and offices at Paddington were also used for formal events; this photograph records the presentation of the St John Ambulance Directors Shield on 27 April 1928. This annual competition for the best ambulance team was keenly contested, and on this occasion was won by a Swindon Works team, standing to the right of the shield. They were (left to right) F. Nutbeam (holding the shield), C. McLeod, L. Mear, S. Edmunds and R. Reeves. The trophy is being presented by the company Chairman, Viscount Churchill, with J. F. Lean and W. G. Chapman, both important figures at Paddington, in attendance.

Apart from the Chief Mechanical Engineer's Department, based at Swindon, and the Signal Department, which was situated at Reading, virtually all other company departments had their headquarters at Paddington. As the scale and scope of the company's operations grew, so did the offices and bureaucracy necessary to service it. Over the years the office complex at the terminus grew extremely large, before being dismantled in more recent years. The headquarters of the Western Region of British Rail was moved to Swindon in the early 1980s, and its privatised successor, Great Western Trains, is still based there rather than at Paddington. This 1904 view of an unidentified office is full of detail, and many of the clerks look very young; on the middle desk a very early typewriter can be seen.

An envelope dating from the 1880s, used for forwarding cash and travel warrants to the Accountants Office at Paddington.

Paddington was also the headquarters of the GWR's publicity office, and this poster was issued by the company in the 1920s.

The General Strike

The political and social instability that followed the end of the First World war finally came to a head in May 1926 with the calling of a General Strike. Out of a total of 111,418 staff employed by the GWR, over 95,000 heeded the call of the union to strike on 5 May, and this figure had only dropped by another 3,000 or so by the end of the dispute nine days later. This meant that practically all of what the company called 'subordinate grades' withdrew their labour, although some emergency arrangements were made to discharge foodstuffs at ports owned by the railway.

Since well over 80 per cent of staff were absent, the Great Western immediately took steps to recruit volunteers to assist. Of the 5,620 who enrolled at Paddington, only 2,234 were utilised, being employed on a variety of tasks; for those wishing to be guards, drivers, firemen and signal staff, special classes were organised. In this photograph volunteers help unload a good train, assisted by the army, whose rifles and kit are piled in the foreground.

GREAT WESTERN RAILWAY.

NOTICE.

Members of the staff who have absented themselves from duty without giving the notice prescribed by the terms of their service are warned that steps are now being taken to fill their places.

FELIX J. C. POLE,
General Manager.

PADDINGTON STATION,
May 10th, 1926.

Above Although of poor quality, this photograph clearly illustrates the fact that trains did run during the strike, even though it was on a much reduced level than normal. On the first day of the strike 392 trains were run all over the system, but this was only 11 per cent of the normal mileage run by the railway. The figure did increase gradually, rising to over 20 per cent of normal mileage towards the end of the strike. Preference was, however, given to suburban traffic rather than the more problematic long-distance services, and this photograph illustrates the arrival of a suburban train on the sixth day of the dispute. Considering the relative inexperience of some volunteers, it is somewhat amazing to record that no serious mishaps occurred during the strike, the General Manager reporting that 16 passengers were shaken but not injured when an auto-train was pushed through the stop blocks at Oswestry.

Left It is thought that this notice was considered rather too inflammatory to issue, so it is not known if it was actually posted on staff noticeboards.

War memorials

No date is given for this staff photograph taken in the board room at Paddington, but it does show the memorial to men killed in the Boer War, which was erected by the company in 1902. Rather less well known than the larger memorial on platform 1, it recorded the names of Great Western men who had lost their lives in the South African campaign. A marble bust of one of the company's most famous servants, Sir Daniel Gooch, peeps over the shoulder of one of the men in the centre of the back row; this statue is now in the collection of the Great Western Railway Museum in Swindon.

The scene on platform 1 at 11.00 am on Armistice Day, 11 November 1920. Wreaths in memory of those killed in the Great War have been laid by representatives of station staff and various other departments, and after the 2-minute silence the thousand or so members of public and staff who had gathered listened to a short address from the Rural Dean of Paddington, the Reverend E. N. Sharpe. The stillness in that great station was, the *GWR Magazine* reported, of 'a most impressive character'. Other services were held elsewhere within the station complex; in the goods station several hundred staff gathered, and hymns were sung to the accompaniment of a small orchestra and choir provided by staff members. A memorial tablet was unveiled by the Chief Accountant Mr R. Cope recording those from his department killed in action. In his address he hoped 'that the sacrifice the men had made would not be in vain'.

The roll of honour seen opposite was one of a series that were erected in stations all over the Great Western network, and in 1922 the much more substantial war memorial featuring the bronze figure of a soldier was unveiled by the company Chairman, Viscount Churchill. The memorial was designed and sculptured by C. S. Jagger RBS; the sculptor had himself fought in the Great War, having been wounded at both Gallipoli and on the Western Front. The architectural setting for the piece was designed by T. S. Tait, a partner in the London firm of Sir John Barnet. Although the memorial featured the figure of a soldier, much was made at the time of the fact that the soldier was portrayed reading a letter from home rather than in a more warlike or aggressive posture. Almost 6,000 people crowded on to the platform to witness the ceremony, which was held, as the previous picture, on Armistice Day.

This view shows the scene some 23 years later, in 1945, when the memorial had been modified to record the loss of Great Western staff in the Second World War. The General Manager, Sir James Milne, is seen performing the unveiling.

5.
ROYAL PADDINGTON

In much of its publicity the Great Western called Paddington its 'Royal Gateway', and with some justification since the station had been much used by royalty over the years, right from the earliest days of the company. It is well known that Queen Victoria travelled by GWR for her first journey by train in 1842, and from then on made considerable use of the railway, the company constructing a Royal Saloon for her in the early 1840s. Since many journeys were taken between Windsor and the capital, it was only fitting that the Queen should have her own facilities at Paddington. This photograph shows the sumptuous interior of the Royal Waiting Room on platform 1. Although used for Royal visitors for many years, it was eventually taken out of use, but has more recently being refurbished, and is now used as a lounge for 1st Class passengers awaiting the departure of trains to the West Country.

Above and below left Paddington station has been the scene of many state and royal occasions, perhaps the most sombre being the funeral of Queen Victoria in 1901. On that day the station was draped with crimson hangings, many arranged carefully to hide the many advertising hoardings that decorated the walls.

This photograph, however, records a rather more cheerful occasion, the return of the Prince of Wales from India in 1922. Flags and buntings have been hung, but nothing on the scale of previous Royal ventures. Station staff have climbed on top of carriage stock to obtain a better view, and some of the staff in the offices are looking down over the balcony of the board room. In the foreground, Their Majesties King George V and Queen Mary and various other officials and retainers await the arrival of the train.

BLOCK H No. 191

GREAT WESTERN RAILWAY,

PADDINGTON STATION.

Funeral of Her Late Majesty the Queen,

SATURDAY, 2ND FEBRUARY, 1901.

ADMIT ONE PERSON TO STAND IN RESERVED ENCLOSURE.

ADMISSION ONLY THROUGH THE BARRIER AT END OF No. 7 PLATFORM.

HOLDERS OF TICKETS SHOULD BE IN THEIR PLACES NOT LATER THAN 10 O'CLOCK.

Right and below The funeral of King George VI on 15 February 1952 was once again the occasion for elaborate arrangements at Paddington; three grandstands were built for invited guests, and the precincts of the station had to be cordoned off for the funeral itself. This photograph must have been taken some hours before the funeral and shows both some of the decorations and the crowd barriers erected on the arrival side of the station. Not surprisingly security is high, and there are a large number of policemen in evidence.

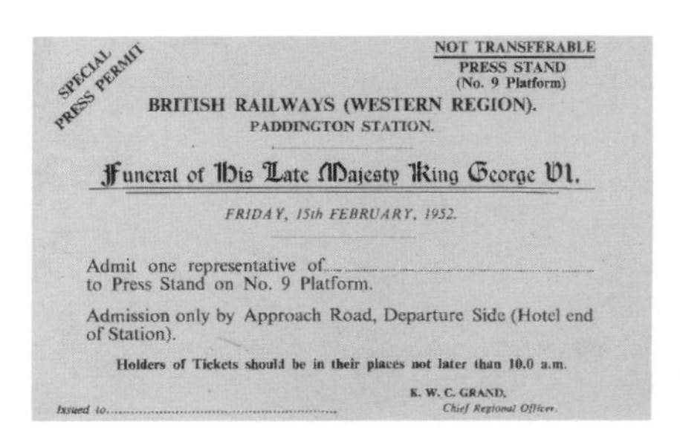

SPECIAL PRESS PERMIT

NOT TRANSFERABLE
PRESS STAND
(No. 9 Platform)

BRITISH RAILWAYS (WESTERN REGION).
PADDINGTON STATION.

Funeral of His Late Majesty King George VI.

FRIDAY, 15th FEBRUARY, 1952.

Admit one representative of ....
to Press Stand on No. 9 Platform.

Admission only by Approach Road, Departure Side (Hotel end of Station).

Holders of Tickets should be in their places not later than 10.0 a.m.

K. W. C. GRAND,
Chief Regional Officer.

Issued to ....

The path of duty was the way to Glory
INWARDS
PARCELS OFFICE

Looking down at the sombre scene from Grandstand 'B', which was located close to the footbridge over platforms 5, 6, 7 and 8; the largest of the three stands, 'A', can be seen between the heavily draped pillars in the left background. The old LNER Royal Train was used for the funeral, and consisted of eight vehicles, comprising a Brake 1st, a '1st Saloon', the Royal Funeral Saloon, saloons for Her Majesty Queen Elizabeth and Her Majesty the Queen Mother, a brake van and two further saloons for the various dignitaries and Royal guests. The locomotive is 'Castle' Class No 4082 *Windsor Castle* - or so it seemed. In fact, *Windsor Castle* was in the middle of an overhaul at Swindon Works when the call came for its use in the funeral arrangements, so Swindon was forced to use subterfuge and exchange the locomotive's nameplates with another member of the class, No 7013 *Bristol Castle*.

A staff notice issued by the company in relation to special trains for the Royal funeral of the Duchess of Connaught and Strathearn, daughter-in-law of Queen Victoria, in 1917.

PRIVATE AND NOT FOR PUBLICATION. Notice No. 9.

GREAT WESTERN RAILWAY.

(For the use of the Railway Servants only.)

NOTICE OF SPECIAL PASSENGER TRAINS

FROM

PADDINGTON TO WINDSOR & ETON

AND BACK,

MONDAY, MARCH 19th, 1917,

for the conveyance of Guests proceeding to the Funeral Service of Her Late Royal Highness the Duchess of Connaught and Strathearn.

FORWARD ARRANGEMENTS.

		A.M.
Paddington (No. 5 Platform) ...	**dep.**	**10.10**
		B. M.L.
Southall	pass	10/22
Slough	pass	10/32
Windsor & Eton (No. 2 Platform) ...	**arr.**	**10.40**

The formation of the Special Train shewn above will be as under:—

Engine
Brake First }
6 Firsts } Cunard Stock. All gangways to be connected.
Brake First }
(All corridors to be on North Side of Train.)

Empty Coaches to leave Old Oak Common at 9.0 a.m. for Paddington.
Train Engine to leave Old Oak Common at 9.35 a.m for Paddington.

B. The 10.5 a.m. Paddington to Windsor & Eton to run via the Relief Line from Friars Junction to Slough. (See also note on Mr. Aldington Royal Train Notice No. 10).

10.15 a.m. PADDINGTON TO PENZANCE.

This train to run at the following amended times between Paddington and Slough:—

		A.M.
Paddington	dep.	10.15
Southall	pass	10/27
Slough	pass	10/38

The Engine of the Special Train also the engine of the Royal Train to run to Slough to turn, in readiness for the return journey from Windsor & Eton.

ALTERED PLATFORM ARRANGEMENTS AT PADDINGTON.

10.5 a.m. Paddington. To start from No. 3 Platform.

7.47 a.m. Aylesbury, due Paddington 9.37 a.m. Must NOT run to No. 5 Platform.

RETURN ARRANGEMENTS.

	No. 1 SPECIAL. (Formed with Royal train coaches and Directors' Saloon.*)		No. 2 SPECIAL. (Formed with Coaches of 10.10 a.m. Special ex. Paddington.
	P.M.		DEP.
Windsor & Eton ... dep. (No. 4 Platform)	**12.50**	**Windsor & Eton ... dep. (No. 2 Platform)**	**1.0**
Slough ... ... pass	12/56 M.L.	Slough ... ... pass	1/6 M.L.
Southall ... ... pass	1/7	Southall ... ... pass	1/17
Paddington ... ... arr. (No. 8 Platform)	**1.20**	**Paddington ... ... arr. (No. 7 Platform)**	**1 30**

* Director's Saloon to be at rear of train with Drawing Room End trailing.

In connection with the running of the above special trains, the following altered working of ordinary trains to operate:—

Windsor portion of 12.5 p.m. Paddington due Windsor 12.43 p.m. to run to No. 1 Platform Line at Windsor.

12.25 p.m. train Paddington to Weymouth to run absolutely to time.

6.
EXPANSION AND IMPROVEMENT

Edwardian developments

These two views show the station before the improvements made just before the Great War. In the first, an unidentified 'Barnum' Class locomotive brings a train of suburban stock away from the terminus. It may be that the carriages are painted in the all-over crimson lake livery used by the company for a short period from 1913 onwards.

A rather gloomy shot of the interior of the station. On the left some of the cast iron pillars supporting the roof can be seen; when the Chief Civil Engineer surveyed the station prior to the addition of another roof span, it was found that stresses on the existing roof had put an enormous strain on the pillars and their foundations. It was thus decided to replace the pillars with more substantial uprights, a process that was interrupted by the Great War and not completed until 1928.

By 1910 traffic at Paddington had increased considerably, and the original Brunel structure was becoming too small to accommodate the extensive services run by the company. For several years before this considerable sums had been spent by the Great Western in demolishing a number of the old brick arch bridges that had choked the track layout leading into the terminus. Replacing these bridges with steel structures left the way open for the expansion of the station itself, and this photograph shows both the station layout before modernisation, and work under way north of the train shed (on the left of the picture) to clear a space for the additional roof span. The jib of a crane can be seen, and a cloud of dust from the building or demolition work. Note also the large number of milk churns on platform 9.

Work began in 1913 on the task of adding another roof span; it was constructed on the site of the old high-level goods yard and the old approach road to the station. Similar in design to the original three built by Brunel, the new span differed only in the fact that it was constructed of steel rather than wrought iron. In the course of the design and construction of this new structure, it was discovered that the smaller original north span (seen on the left of this picture) had been pushed considerably out of true by the other two parts of the train shed. A discrepancy of over 5 inches meant that the new roof would act as a counterbalance to the rest of the structure. Work is well advanced in this 1916 view of the arrival side of the station. On the left are the rather scruffy offices that would be replaced by a much more substantial office block in the 1930s.

An aerial view of the station taken in the 1920s after the completion of the new roof span, but before the rebuilding work and improvements that took place in the early 1930s. Some impression of the size of the offices at Paddington can clearly be seen in this picture, since they stretch the whole length of the station on the departure side.

Interwar improvements

Although the Great Western had begun the task of modernising the station just before the onset of the Great War, the increases in traffic experienced by the company meant that the addition of the extra roof span and extra platform space was not enough. A report to the General Manager in 1927 noted that Paddington had 'passed the stage where minor alterations and additions can improve its working, and that in fact . . . entire reorganisation and a measure of expansion must be put in hand if matters are to be prevented from going from bad to worse.' All the measures suggested added up to over £2 million in expenditure, and ultimately lack of capital, the effects of the Depression and eventually the war led to some of the more ambitious proposals not being completed.

One of the major items identified in the report was the lack of parcels accommodation; the circulating area behind the platforms known as the Lawn had become increasingly cramped and crowded. Not only did passengers have to contend with barrows, trolleys and piles of parcels, as this photograph clearly illustrates, but also the horse and motor vehicles that delivered the goods. From this view it is clear that the view greeting the passenger visiting the Great Western's most prestigious station was not the most scenic. There are over 25 staff at work here, and as well as the enormous pile of parcels being processed, some of the other clutter that dominated the area behind the buffer stops can also be clearly seen.

A new facility for the handling of this traffic thus became an urgent priority. The Development (Loans, Guarantees & Grants) Act of 1929 provided £1 million for redevelopment work, and land was acquired in Bishop's Road to allow for a new Parcels Depot to be built, extending platform 1 to become platform 1A. This atmospheric photograph taken in 1929 shows the land behind Bishop's Bridge Road that the company purchased for this purpose before demolition took place. To assist the movement of barrows, a new subway was constructed under the arrival approach road, which linked the new depot with the existing subways under the platforms.

POST OFFICE
THE
1,062 PAGES
8,000 ADDRESSES
ARRIVAL INDICATOR
ARRIVALS
DEPARTURES
NOW IS THE TIME
TO PURCHASE YOUR HOUSE
THE
WESTBOURNE PARK
BUILDING SOCIETY
WILL ASSIST YOU ON LOWEST TERMS
WESTBOURNE HOUSE
WESTBOURNE GROVE W.2
TWO MINUTES FROM THIS STATION
HYDRO HOTEL
FALMOUTH
Boots

Above left The transformation of the Lawn is most apparent in this August 1935 photograph, which shows it as a light, spacious and pleasant circulating area for passengers. Reporting the rebuilding of the Lawn in 1931, one newspaper noted that 'soon that favourite meeting place of sweethearts . . . will have changed from "under the clock" on platform 1, to the "Lounge on the lawn"'.

Once parcels traffic had been moved to the new depot, the company could also make other improvements. The ugly cast iron columns and short-span roof were removed, and a new more modern three-bay roof substituted. Considerable work was also done to upgrade the lighting of the area, and large 'Mazdalux' lamps were installed. Other changes included a new entrance to the Great Western Royal Hotel, and refurbishment of offices and the cloakroom on platform 1. The entrance to both the Bakerloo and Metropolitan Underground stations was also upgraded. The year 1935 was the centenary of the Great Western Railway, and advertisements for the special anniversary supplement to *The Times* newspaper can be seen above the Lawn area.

Left In March 1934 the Great Western installed a new Train Indicator in the centre of the Lawn. This imposing structure was constructed of polished teak, and consisted of eight panels showing train arrivals, with departures being listed on the other side. The mechanism used to operate the indicator was built by Siemens Ltd and used a very primitive computer system whereby information for each train for a particular day was stored on what the company described as 'Magazines', which could be called up by an operator located in an office away from the Lawn. This photograph shows the scene at 3.45 in the afternoon; three of the trains indicated are running late, with the Taunton train due at 4.05 thought to be 11 minutes behind time. Underneath the indicator there are three posters advertising the 1934 edition of 'Holiday Haunts', priced at 6d.

Above From this December 1935 photograph of the Lawn it seems that considerable efforts have been made to give the area a seasonal flavour. The roof above the concourse has been transformed into a 'starry sky' and an 18-foot-high windmill has been decorated with what the *GWR Magazine* called 'bon-bons'. In front of each pillar stood 10-foot-high toy soldiers, and girders were festooned with garlands of holly and 'scintillating' coloured chains, the report noted. The large Christmas cracker reads '100th Christmas', a reference no doubt to the company's centenary celebrations that had dominated the year. No expense was spared and the display was completed with the addition of 500 additional lights that floodlit the decorations. In the background an illuminated sign indicates the entrance to the Great Western Royal Hotel.

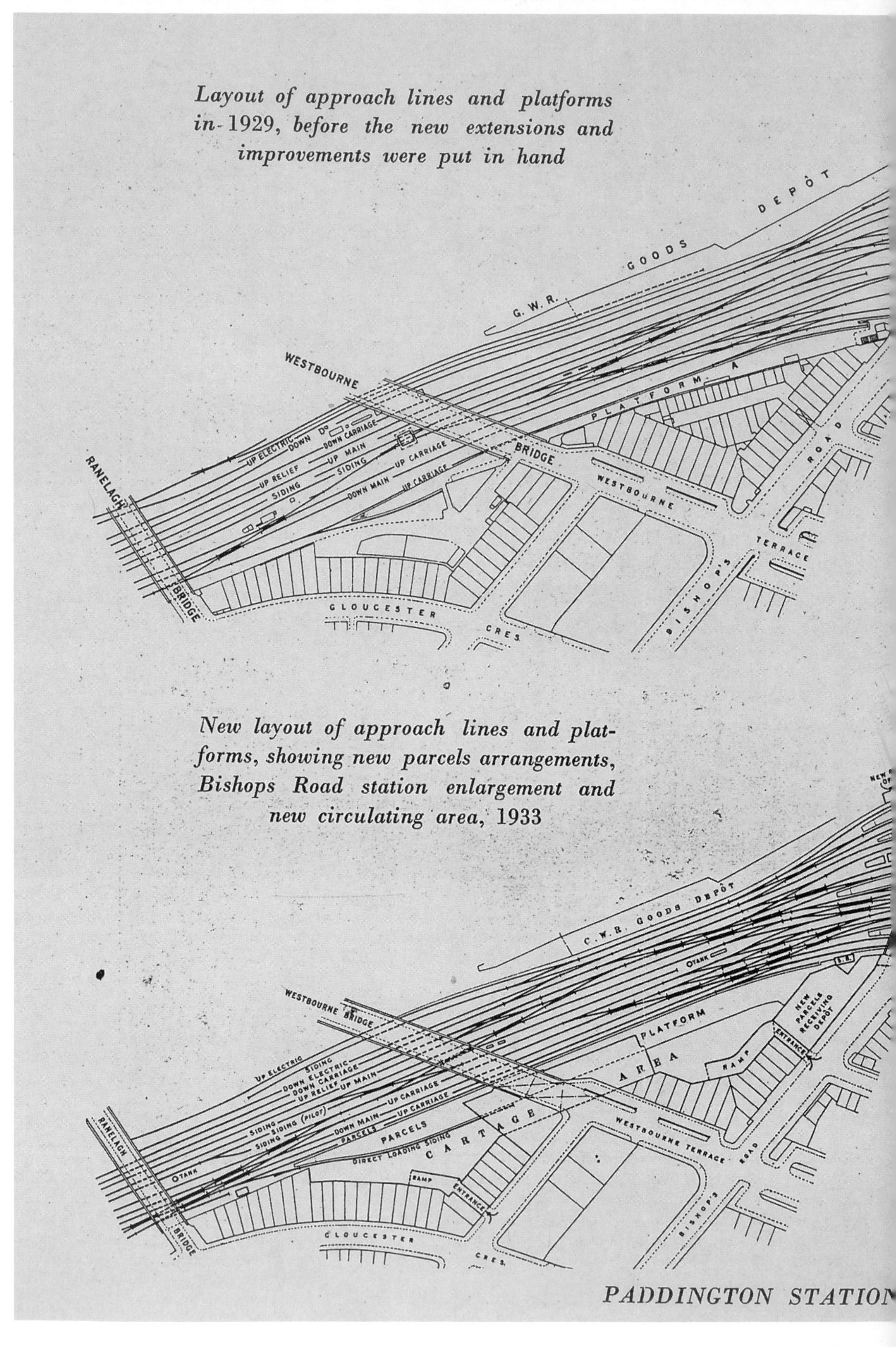

'Before and after' plans of the station from the

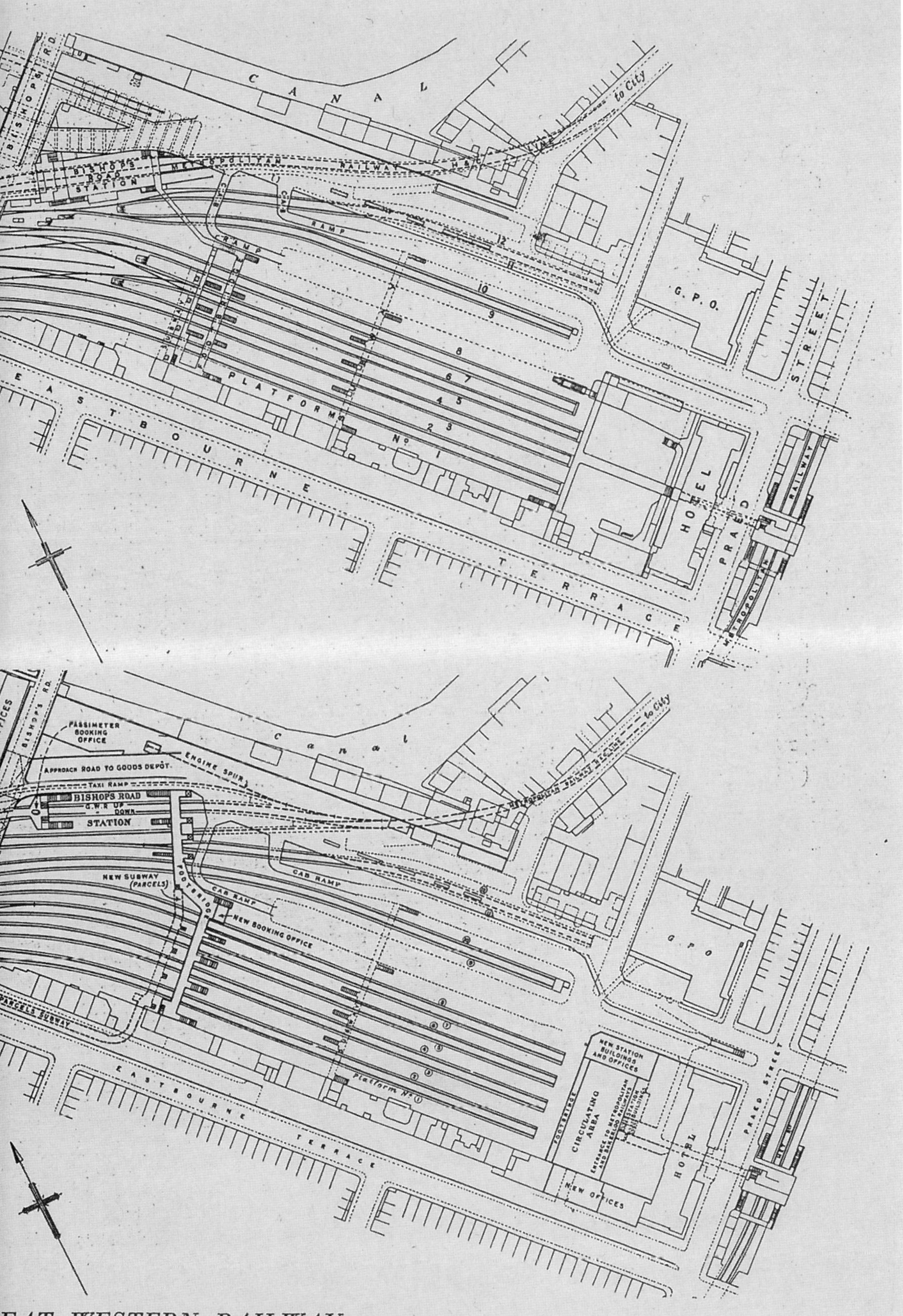

3 December 1933 edition of *The Railway Gazette*.

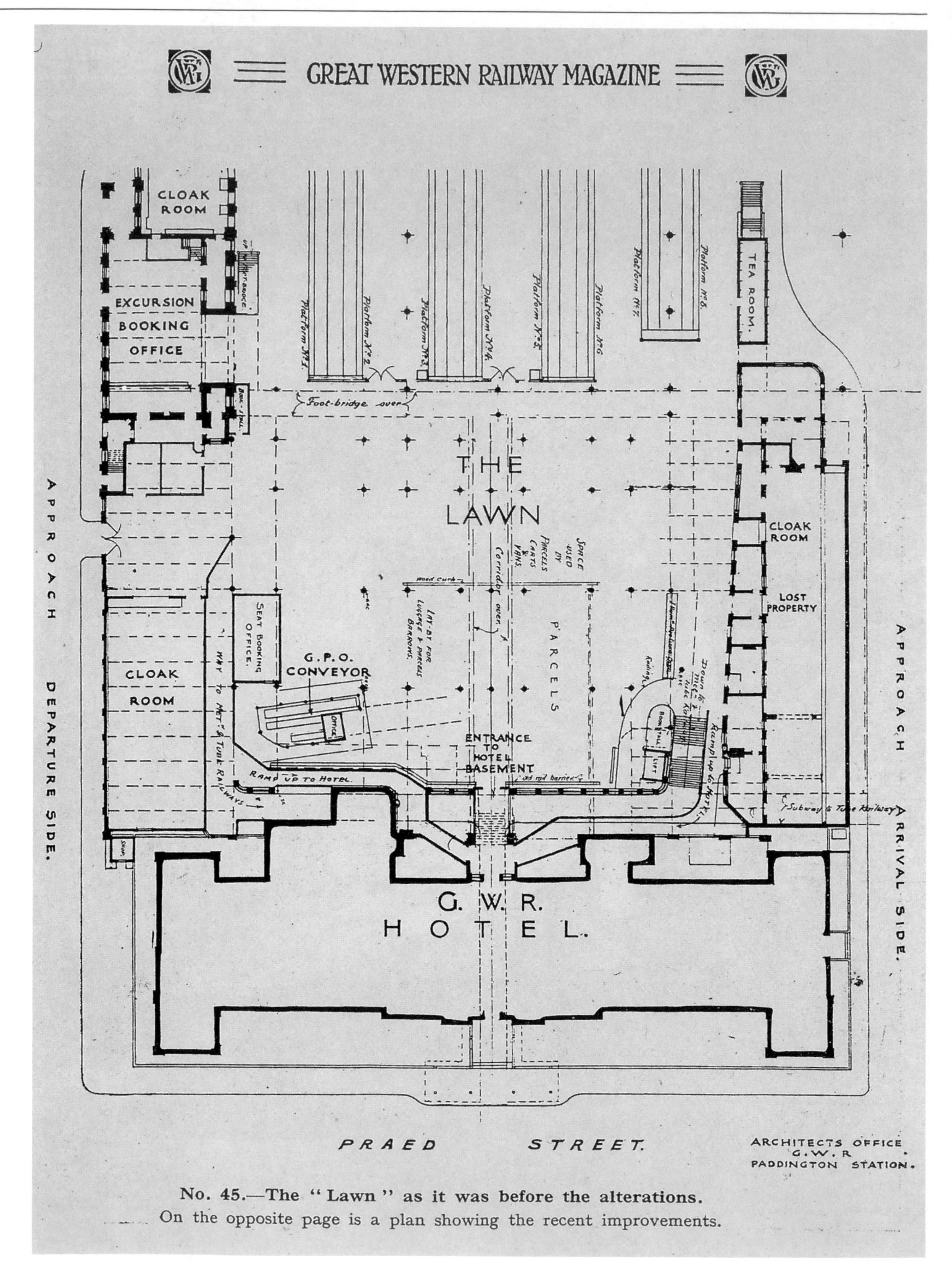

No. 45.—The "Lawn" as it was before the alterations.
On the opposite page is a plan showing the recent improvements.

Plans of the Lawn before and after modernisation,

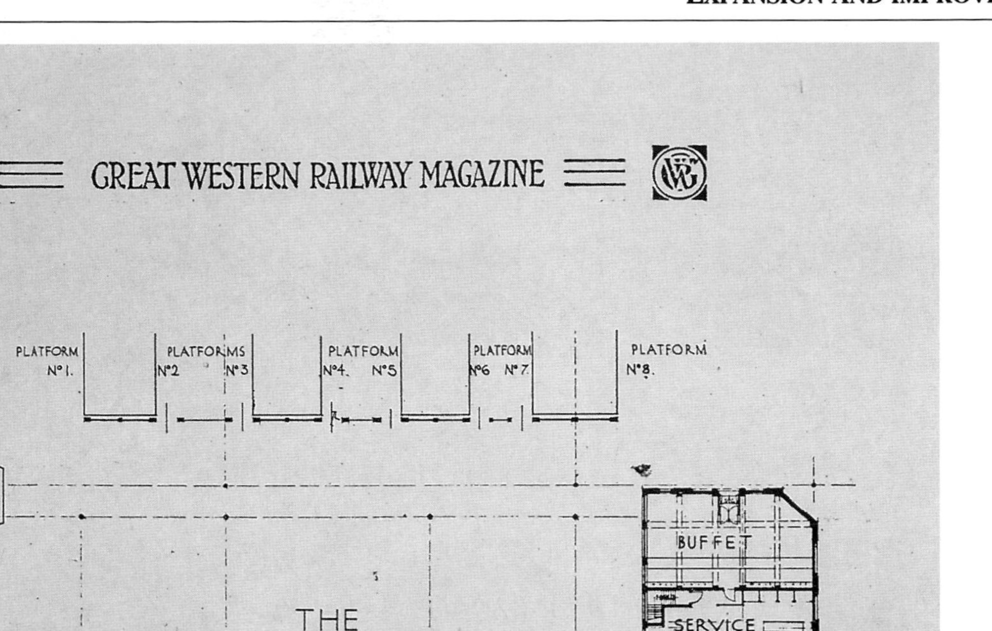

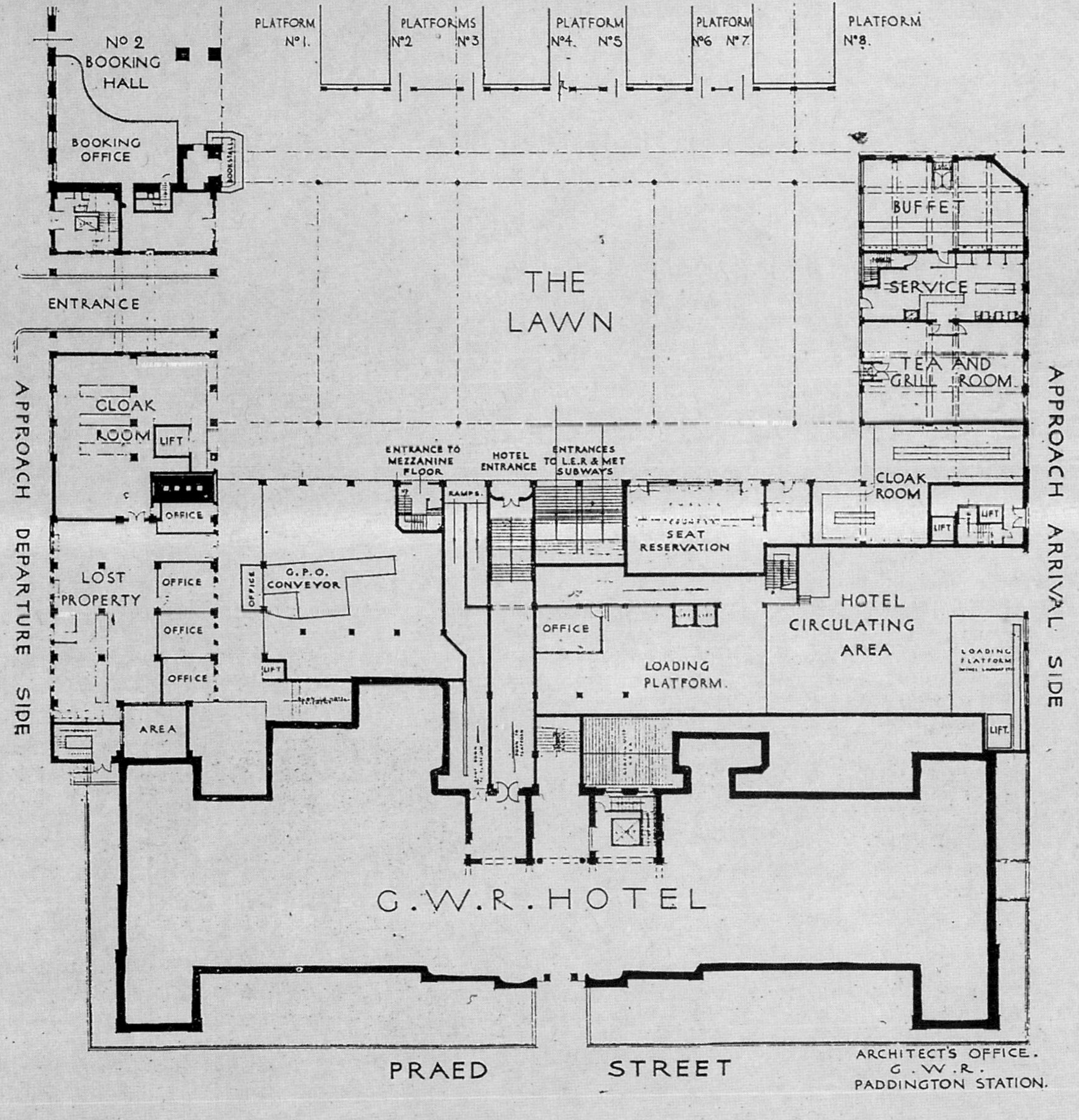

No. 46.—The "Lawn" as it is to-day.

This plan illustrates the clearance made to the "Lawn," forming the new concourse. It will be noticed that the buffer stops have been moved back, and gates and railings placed across this end of the "Lawn." The new entrance to the Subways of the Bakerloo and Metropolitan Railways is shown, as well as the Hotel Circulating Area off the Arrival Side Approach Road, and the new corridor and entrance to the Hotel from the "Lawn."

71

taken from the *Great Western Railway Magazine*.

Another task completed before the outbreak of the Second World war was the lengthening of the platforms at Paddington; the platform surface was made up of precast concrete sections that could be laid quickly and without too much disruption to train services. The task was completed by the construction of awnings to protect passengers from the weather, a job that seems well in hand in this photograph.

Despite the fast services run by the Great Western in the years between the two World Wars, a Bristol firm, E. Jones & Sons, thought that they could run a competing motor bus service between London and Bristol. This photograph, taken in April 1928, shows the scene just around the corner from Paddington station, with passengers about to depart. How long this particular rival service lasted is not recorded, but at this time it would not have been much of a threat. The situation in more recent times has been somewhat different, however.

7.
PADDINGTON AT WAR

The scene at Paddington on 29 September 1938, when the Great Western Railway carried out an evacuation exercise as a result of the Munich Crisis. Tension in Europe had been rising for some considerable time, and the threat of war in Czechoslovakia led to the mobilisation of the fleet on 26 September. With the very real threat of another war in Europe, the GWR participated in an exercise that involved the running of over 200 trains to evacuate school children, hospital patients and other vulnerable groups. In the event, the return of the Prime Minister Neville Chamberlain from Munich with the peace accord that, he promised, would give 'peace in our time' meant that tension was reduced at least for the present. The added complication of having to run troop trains and other special freight workings related to the armed forces meant that in the event the company learned much from the experience, which they were to repeat for real less than a year later.

When war was declared on 3 September 1939 the Great Western already had a well-rehearsed evacuation programme from both the capital and other major cities such as Birmingham. Arrangements for the evacuation of children had been planned well in advance of the announcement by the Ministry of Health on 31 August that children should be moved to country areas as a precautionary measure, and timetables had been printed some weeks before this. Over a four-day period some 112,994 evacuees were carried by the GWR from the London area; this very posed photograph, no doubt taken for propaganda purposes, shows a group of nurses waving off children from the terminus. The nurses may well have been Great Western employees, since the company arranged for staff with St John Ambulance qualifications to be in attendance at all major departure and arrival stations.

Almost all the evacuees moved by the Great Western were in fact transported not from Paddington, but from Acton and Ealing Broadway stations, which had rather better Underground connections; since many children were coming in school groups from all over London, this was obviously an important consideration. Some idea of the scale of movement from Paddington as compared to Ealing may be gained from the fact that only 850 per day were dispatched from Paddington as opposed to over 46,500 per day from Ealing! In this view children emerge from the subway on to platform 5, complete with accompanying nurse.

Despite the small number of children moved from Paddington during the evacuation programme, it was a far better place to obtain publicity photographs. The author has not been able to locate any pictures taken at the two smaller Great Western stations involved, but there are a good number taken at the terminus. Here a railway policewoman is checking the labels attached to each evacuee. Although some photographs taken of the evacuation are obviously posed, it is not difficult to be moved by the faces of the children themselves, whose smiles betray the unhappiness and anxiety that being separated from their parents entailed.

Left The first two days of the evacuation programme concentrated mainly on the movement of schoolchildren, with the remaining two days devoted to the dispatch of mothers with children and the sick. In all the company ran 164 trains to all parts of the Great Western network, with evacuees being moved as far west as Cornwall, and as near as Thames Valley locations such as Maidenhead. In true GWR fashion, the evacuation programme ran like a well-oiled military operation, and was repeated by all the other major railways, moving in all a total of 1,334,358 children, parents, teachers and hospital patients. This photograph was probably taken on either the third or fourth day of the programme, when mothers with young children were moved to safer locations.

Below left When the emphasis of German Luftwaffe attacks changed from the targeting of RAF bases to Britain's cities, damage to Great Western property was inevitable. Paddington, being in the heart of London, suffered considerable damage in the Blitz, but, considering its size, survived the war relatively unscathed. Most of the pictures shown in this section were taken by Mr R. C. Kirkpatrick, who worked for the company's Civil Engineer's Department. Although only snapshots, they contrast strongly with 'official' pictures taken at the time, which only hint at some of the damage done.

This picture, taken from a window of the Great Western Royal Hotel, shows the damage done to the glazing of the roof and the offices on 17 April 1941 when a land mine (also known as a parachute mine) exploded in the departure road of the station next to platform 1. A large hole can be seen in the roof of the offices to the left of the picture, and demolition was necessary to make the area safe.

Above right The parachute mine caused enormous damage to facilities on the departure side of the station; the No 2 Booking Office was wrecked, as was property belonging to Wymans, Boots the Chemist and Lyons. Damage to offices above caused debris to fall down into the waiting room on platform 1, which was unfortunately kept open all night; some passengers sheltering there were trapped in the rubble, and despite the efforts of rescue teams a number were killed. In all 18 people were killed in the incident, including six staff; a further 97 were injured. With such a high number of casualties, GWR rescue and first aid staff needed the assistance of Paddington Borough Council rescue teams and a detachment of Auxiliary Military Pioneer Corps.

Paddington Station 22.3.44
No. 425
CRATER

Paddington Station 22.3.44
No. 425

Above left On the night of 22 March 1944 Paddington experienced its 425th incident of the war, when a 500 kg bomb pierced Brunel's roof and landed between platforms 6 and 7. The following photographs show something of the speed at which clearing up took place, and how Great Western staff coped with the emergency. The bomb fell at 1.00 am and this picture shows the scene 7 hours later with clearing-up work already well under way.

Left Amazingly the bomb crater was filled in by 1.00 pm the same day, and this photograph shows work well in hand to relay the trackwork destroyed by the bomb. A handwritten caption on the back of the photograph records that all tracks were joined up by 6.30 pm on the 22nd, meaning that trains could run again less than 24 hours after the air raid.

Above Although the bomb crater in the heart of the station was serious, what was perhaps more serious was the damage to the Brunel roof. This picture, although of poor quality, shows the serious damage to the wrought iron structure and was titled by the photographer 'Brunel's broken rib'.

Paddington Station
22.3.44
No425

Paddington Station
22.3.44

Above left Although work had started to clear the debris at ground level, it was not so easy to make repairs to the roof. It was necessary to erect a large trestle to enable workmen to clear any dangerous material and to make safe the roof. This was not an easy process, and this photograph was not taken until 12.30 pm on 25 March, three days after the raid. A steam crane has been brought into the station to lift scaffolding and other material up to the level of the top deck.

Left A photograph taken some three months later, on 25 July 1944, when Brunel's 'broken rib' had been finally repaired. Looking down the station, temporary repairs to the glass screens on the front of the train shed can also be seen, no doubt necessary because of blast damage.

Top Ministry of Home Security officials inspecting a hole in the taxi rank over platform 11 at Paddington on 22 March 1944. This was a result of an unexploded 500 kg bomb that fell during the same raid as the one described in the previous photographs. Unexploded bombs caused chaos to the Great Western and other railway companies, since the delays created often disrupted services as much as actual bomb damage.

POST CARD.

ADDRESS ONLY.

The General Manager,
Claims Section,
Great Western Railway Company,
Beenham Grange,
~~Paddington Station~~,
Aldermaston, Berks.
~~London, W.2~~.

Above Evidence that much of the administration done at Paddington before the war was done subsequently at Beenham Grange, where a large proportion of the staff had been evacuated for the duration.

The pictures illustrating the clearing-up operations done by company staff after air raids highlighted the long and difficult nature of the work. This 21-foot-long mobile trailer canteen was designed by the Great Western's Road Transport Department at Slough, and built at Swindon in the Carriage Works. Hauled by a Bedford Scammell 6/8 ton articulated tractor unit, the canteen was well equipped with a 125-gallon water tank to keep the tea urn well supplied. Normally staffed by a driver and attendant, the vehicle also carried stocks of dried food so that snacks and hot drinks could be provided for GWR staff who, as a result of bombing, might not be able to obtain food.

The final picture in this section shows a female member of staff busy sticking one of the best-known posters of the Second World War on to a wall at Paddington. As the war progressed, and the need to conscript more men into the armed forces increased, so the number of women employed by the Great Western grew, so that by 1943 there were over 16,000 doing all manner of tasks. In a 1943 article in the *GWR Magazine*, a correspondent reported that women were more than capable of doing even the heaviest work, and that 'once women become accustomed to their . . . jobs, they like their work and carry on very successfully with their wartime tasks'. This last sentence leaves the reader in no doubt that when the men returned from the war, women would be expected to return to domestic duties!

8. THE MODERN ERA

Advent of the diesels

Below The second of the two pioneering gas turbine locomotives purchased by the Western Region of British Railways, No 18100, was more conventional in appearance than its sister locomotive No 18000, nicknamed 'Kerosene Castle' by Swindon staff. No 18100 had in fact been ordered before the latter locomotive, but was not delivered by its manufacturer, Metropolitan Vickers Ltd, until late in December 1951. A press launch was held at Paddington on 29 January 1952 to preview the new engine, but no special run was held on that day, since it was yet to complete trials on the main line. As it was, the locomotive managed to disgrace itself (as had No 18000), the power of its exhaust dislodging large quantities of soot from the station roof on to passengers below. For the next couple of weeks it was engaged on trials hauling either the 11.15 Paddington-Bristol service, or the 11.00 Paddington-Plymouth train; this undated picture probably originates from one of these trial runs.

Above right A rather scruffy 'Castle' Class locomotive contrasts with the gleaming paintwork of 'Warship' Class diesel-hydraulic locomotive No D601 *Ark Royal*, photographed leaving Paddington on 6 August 1958 with a down parcels train. This locomotive was one of the original batch of this class built in 1957 by the North British Locomotive Company, which were never as successful as the larger and more powerful locomotives that followed from Swindon. When the more powerful D800 'Warship' Class was introduced, having two classes with the same name not surprisingly caused some confusion.

Below right Diesel-hydraulic locomotive No D800 *Sir Brian Robertson* waits to leave Paddington on the 'Cornish Riviera Express' service in 1958. The 2,200 hp engines of this second class of 'Warships' made them much more powerful than the D600 series. The design of this and the 'Western' Class that was to follow was ultimately the last gesture of defiance from Swindon in 'going its own way'. Rather than use diesel-electric transmission, which had been adopted by other Regions, the WR decided to adapt a diesel-hydraulic unit pioneered by the state railways in West Germany. The streamlined exterior was also innovative, and the end product was an attractive and reliable locomotive, 38 of which were built between 1957 and 1961.

180
D601
CORNISH RIVIERA EXPRESS
FIRST 2,200 H.P.
DIESEL HYDRAULIC
LOCOMOTIVE
BUILT IN BRITISH RAILWAYS WORKSHOPS
D800

The 'Warships', although useful, proved to be insufficiently powerful for the heavier express services run on Western Region, so Swindon produced a larger 2,750 hp locomotive, again with diesel-hydraulic transmission. Thirty of the 'Western' D1000 Class locomotives were actually built at Swindon, although others were built at Crewe. The identity of this filthy 'Western' is not recorded in this photograph, taken in February 1966 showing two drivers modelling new uniforms at Paddington.

Other familiar sights at Paddington in the 1960s were the Blue Pullman trains, which ran mainly on services between Paddington and Bristol. This photograph, taken from platform 1 on 17 April 1964, shows a Pullman train waiting in platform 4. The lack of rolling-stock in the nearest two platforms allows one to see the unusual track formation, which with its transverse sleepering and tiebars at intervals is reminiscent of broad gauge baulk road. The station is almost deserted, which also shows off the lines of Brunel's original train shed to their best advantage, over a hundred years after construction.

Present and future

With the end of steam on British Rail's Western Region, far-reaching changes were made at Paddington. The old arrangements for operating the station, which as already mentioned had meant that platforms 1 to 4 could only be used for departures and 7 to 11 for arrivals, had hampered the operation of an efficient station, with the turn-round of stock from arrival to departure being around 2 hours. The new arrangements allowed for a 40-minute turn-round and involved a drastic remodelling of the track layout, a new signalling system, allowing in-and-out working on all platform roads, and other work such as the installation of heaters on 96 points to prevent the freezing of the mechanisms in cold weather. This photograph, taken in November 1967, shows the scene just outside the station, with new trackwork being installed. During that month half the station was closed, and West Country and Birmingham trains were diverted to Kensington Olympia station.

This is a 1970 view down from the footbridge linking platforms 1 to 8. Other work done during the modernisation of the station included the lowering of tracks on the arrival side, and the standardisation of platform heights at 3 feet. A new lighting system was also installed, and this night scene shows Brunel's roof illuminated by new lamps, while below a sleeper service awaits departure. On the far left newspaper vans are much in evidence, which suggests that the picture must have been taken late at night.

Right Passengers admire the lines of one of the two prototype High Speed Train power cars built by British Rail in 1972. In an effort to create a more efficient high-speed intercity service, BR introduced the concept of double-ended trains, much like the Blue Pullman concept. The prototype set was tested extensively on the Western Region, and in 1976 production HST services commenced in earnest. Locomotive-hauled passenger trains are now very rare, and HSTs are still the mainstay of the Great Western main line. One of the original two power cars, No 41001, has been preserved by the National Railway Museum at York.

Below In its heyday the Great Western spent considerable sums lengthening the platforms at Paddington to enable longer trains to be accommodated. In the 1970s this process was reversed when the passenger circulating area on the Lawn was increased. Ticket barriers were moved about 37 metres westwards and a new train indicator board was provided. The process of change is constant, with new shop units being introduced in more recent years; perhaps the most significant improvement to the station has been the refurbishment of the Brunel train shed. Substantial investment by British Rail and the Railway Heritage Trust ensured that the complete overhaul of the roof was done to the highest standard, ensuring the survival of the building for future generations of railway travellers. This 1979 photograph shows the scene at Paddington during the celebrations held to mark the 125th anniversary celebrations; the steam of a Great Western locomotive can faintly be seen on the extreme right of the picture.

Another new era at Paddington. In February 1996 one of the first new franchises of the newly privatised railway was awarded to Great Western Trains, and this photograph shows the first two High Speed Trains painted in the new company livery. The power units make a fine sight under the roof of Brunel's magnificent train shed, and form a fitting finale to this book.

A view of the rather cluttered area in front of the Brunel train shed at Paddington, with only one High Speed Train in sight. The landscape around the station has certainly changed somewhat in the more recent past, with office blocks now part of the skyline. Over 150 years after its construction, Paddington is still carrying out the job it was built to do; it is still London's Gateway to the West, and long may it continue to be so.

INDEX